Reinhold Niebuhr's Apologetics

by

Donald G. Bloesch

Doctoral dissertation, 1956
University of Chicago
Revised version, 2002

Wipf and Stock Publishers
EUGENE, OREGON

Wipf and Stock Publishers
199 W 8th Ave, Suite 3
Eugene, OR 97401

Reinhold Niebuhr's Apologetics
By Bloesch, Donald G.
Copyright© by Bloesch, Brenda
ISBN 13: 978-1-57910-963-9
Publication date 5/15/2002

Dedicated to my
thesis advisors:

Bernard E. Meland
James Hastings Nichols
J. Coert Rylaarsdam

Table of Contents

Foreword to Revised Version i

Prologue 1

I. *Introduction* 3
    Two Types of Theology 3
    Statement of Thesis 11

II. *Niebuhr's Break with Traditional Apologetics* 17
    Background of Niebuhr's Polemic 17
    Analysis of Syncretic Theology 24
    Attitude Towards Other Kinds of Apologetics 32

III. *Niebuhr's Vindication of the Apologetic Principle* 35
    General Revelation 35
    Dialectical Theology 39
    Existential Disruption 44

IV. *Apologetics as a Means of Validating the Faith* 51
    Negative Validation 52
    Positive Validation 57
    Relation of Apologetics to Commitment 62

V. A Critique of Niebuhr's Methodology 73
- The Authority of the Bible 73
- Methodological Principles 82
- Niebuhr's Anthropology 89
- Niebuhr on the Means of Grace 100
- The Apologetic Principle 106

VI. A New Role for Apologetics 111
- The Mission of the Church 111
- Faith Seeking Understanding 117
- Apologetics as a Subsidiary of Kerygmatic Theology 122
- Apologetics as an Aid in Witnessing 134

Epilogue 145

Foreword to Revised Version

I had not previously planned to publish my doctoral thesis on Reinhold Niebuhr mainly because my thinking at the time of its completion (June, 1956) was in a state of flux, and I thought it better to wait until I had arrived at a fuller perspective on some of the issues relating to the communication of the gospel to an unbelieving world. In addition Reinhold Niebuhr was a warm friend of my father's and an active member of the same denomination – the Evangelical Synod of North America, later the Evangelical and Reformed Church.[1] I was therefore reluctant to take public issue with this theological mentor on a question so integral to his theology – the role of apologetics in the church's mission. This is not to deny the fact that I have learned from him positively in so many areas of theology. His keen perception of the tensions between love and justice, for example, can be appreciated by all theologians who wish to be biblical and evangelical. Moreover, through the years I have given critiques of various facets of Niebuhr's thought and did not believe my thesis would substantially add to this evaluation.[2] Now, however, I believe the publication of this particular thesis could be valuable, first to those who are delving into my own thought on some of these issues, and second because of the renewed and growing interest in apologetics, especially in conservative Protestant circles.[3]

---

[1] Since 1957 this church has formed a part of the United Church of Christ.

[2] See Donald G. Bloesch, *The Christian Witness in a Secular Age* (Minneapolis: Augsburg, 1968), pp. 63-72; and Bloesch, *Freedom for Obedience* (San Francisco: Harper & Row, 1987), pp. 100-105; 116-117.

[3] See, for example, William A. Dembski and Jay Wesley Richards, ed., *Unapologetic Apologetics* (Downers Grove, IL: InterVarsity Press, 2001).

I cannot but admire Niebuhr's prodigious effort to establish the credibility of the Christian religion in a secular culture. It should be noted that Niebuhr did gain a certain following among the intelligentsia, though the number who were actually moved to embrace the Christian faith through his apologetic forays was probably very small. Some of his secular peers acknowledged the cogency of his arguments for original sin, but they were not thereby convinced that the solution to the human quandary is faith in Jesus Christ.

Niebuhr sought to appeal to the intellectual community by presenting an analysis of the human predicament that would resonate with their deepest insights on human life and destiny. In his sermons in particular he tried to show that human hubris leads ineluctably to divine retribution and that our only hope is trust in the mercy and forbearance of the God revealed in biblical history and preeminently in Jesus Christ.

Niebuhr's apologetic strategy was to move unbelieving humanity toward faith in Christ by exposing the fallacies and illusions that form the basis of their present commitments. The critical question is whether in the light of Holy Scripture people come to faith in this way. St. Paul apparently did not think so, since he was adamant that faith comes only through being confronted by the message of the cross, and this we know primarily through preaching (cf. Rom. 10:14-17; I Cor. 1:21; II Thes. 2:14). Paul was convinced that the natural person or the unspiritual person does not receive the gifts of the Spirit, "for they are folly to him" (I Cor. 2:14). To be sure Paul seemed to embrace an apologetic stance in his sermon to the Athenians (Ac. 17:22-31). While I argue in my thesis that Paul realized he had been mistaken in his apologetic approach to the academics in Athens, I am now inclined to believe that Paul did not specifically offer an apology for faith. Instead he presented a sermon that began with the doctrine of creation and culminated in the proclamation of the cross and resurrection. Nevertheless Paul apparently changed his emphasis when he embarked on his evangelistic mission to Corinth, since he then resolved to know nothing but Jesus Christ and him crucified (I Cor. 2:2). It can also be disputed that Paul appealed to a point of contact with Greek thought when he referred to the Athenian altar to an unknown God. My position is that this was not a theological but a sociological point of contact. This is to say, he did not build his theology upon his listeners' faint recollections of spiritual truth; this reference to the unknown God was simply a device to gain their attention.

Whereas in my thesis I took a neo-Lutheran view that seemed to bind the Spirit of God to the means of grace, particularly the sermon, I would now emphasize the freedom of God to use many different means or no visible means at all in bringing people to faith. At the same time, I believe that God is faithful to His Word and that He has promised to speak when people uphold His name and proclaim His plan of salvation.

In my theological maturity I would now resist reducing the mission of the church to kerygmatic proclamation. With Niebuhr I would uphold various means of grace, but nonetheless still insist on the primacy of the preached word. Yet I would stress the fact that the proclaimed word includes more than the gospel or the kerygma: it also comprises the law of God – the call to discipleship under the cross. The whole counsel of God is not the kerygma, not even the gospel (the divine content of the kerygma) but God's commandment as well, and this is a commandment always addressed to the concrete situation in which people find themselves. Instead of either a kerygmatic theology of proclamation or an apologetic theology of rational persuasion I now uphold a theology of Word and Spirit in which the Spirit interprets the Word and applies the Word to the contemporary social matrix – the situation to which the Word is directed. The Spirit also confirms the truth of faith in our hearts when we hear it proclaimed and see it enacted in life.

I no longer define the mission of the church as simply the confession of what God has done for us in Christ, the upholding of the name of Christ before the world. This mission also includes bringing people to faith; it is not simply making the truth of faith known. I was perhaps too Barthian in my thesis, possibly in reaction to Niebuhr, and thereby made little place for the winning of souls to the kingdom.

While pursuing my ministerial and doctoral degrees at the University of Chicago, I was close to Niebuhr in entertaining the viability of a biblical, existentialist theology in which despair is the precursor of faith. Yet I was not entirely comfortable with this Kierkegaardian approach, and in subsequent years I have tried to move beyond existentialism to the wisdom of the fathers of the faith. I believe Niebuhr too was moving in this direction – toward an evangelical catholicity in which the Reformation is united not with Renaissance ideas (Niebuhr's goal in his *Nature and Destiny of Man*) but with the insights of the saints and sages of the church universal. It is significant that in his later years Niebuhr was more willing to describe himself as an Augustinian than as either a Lutheran or a Calvinist.

I remain indebted to Niebuhr for his vigorous defense of paradox in Christian faith and for his welcome admission of mystery in divine revelation. He made a valiant effort to transcend the polarity between rationalism, in which mystery is reduced to logic, and mysticism, in which meaning is dissolved in mystery. He staunchly affirmed a rational faith but one that at the same time transcends the parameters of reason. This is also my goal in theology.

Niebuhr was equally unhappy with the monergism of the Reformers, in which grace does all, and the synergism of the Catholic semi-Pelagian tradition, in which God and His human creation cooperate in the procuring of salvation. With Niebuhr I affirm the paradoxical unity of human causality and divine concurrence. Niebuhr sometimes lapsed into synergism, perhaps out of opposition to a divine monergism associated with the Reformers and Karl Barth. If he were living today I am confident that he would at least be open to endorsing my third alternative – the mystery of double agency in which God does all, but in this action the human subject is enabled and motivated to follow in faith and obedience.

I still remain committed to the baptism of secular and philosophical concepts and images into the service of the gospel. But I confess that at least at one point in my thesis I manifested a subtle capitulation to the culture of democratic egalitarianism by being willing to jettison the biblical symbol of "king" in reference to the living God because of the cultural bias against monarchy (p. 139). Sometimes we need to emphasize precisely those symbols that underscore the contradiction between the claims of faith and the aspirations of the culture.

From Emil Brunner I borrowed the term "believing integration" to describe the apologetic task in its new role, but I would insist that this is an apologetics within dogmatics or even better a dogmatics with an apologetic element. In contrast to Brunner I do not make a place for a natural theology that is distinct from a theology of revelation. Niebuhr, it is interesting to note, found himself much closer to Brunner than to Barth in this whole area of the communication of the gospel to the unbelieving world. I would say with Barth that the best apologetics is a good dogmatics.

With Barth and against Niebuhr I contend that unbelief must not be taken too seriously in view of the fact that God's hand is in all of human history. Yet with Niebuhr I am convinced that there is still a place for combating unbelief, since through unbelief people can be turned toward damnation. Yet in warning against unbelief we must not paint a picture that is overly bleak, since God's grace is greater than human sin, the Spirit of God is more powerful than the powers of the world. Niebuhr has said that we must be provisionally pessimistic because of original sin and ultimately optimistic because of the sovereignty of divine grace. I contend that even in our pessimism we must be optimistic because of the biblical thesis that God is in control even when the devils seem to run rampant.

Carl F.H. Henry gave this salutary advice to his students: "Strike a blow in defense of the gospel." This blow, however, must not be construed as undercutting the rational supports of systems of unbelief, for this can only drive people into despair, not a creative despair that supposedly leads to faith, but a destructive despair –

the fruit of sin against a holy God. We strike a blow for the gospel when we confess the name of Christ and tell the story of the salvation of Christ. To be sure in accomplishing this task we need to enter the thought world of our hearers, but with the knowledge that the gospel of God, which is always God's possession , cannot be united with the ideological constructs of our hearers. These constructs like the idols of old must be torn down, but it is the gospel itself which does this iconoclastic work, not the strategies of the apologist, however impressive.

Niebuhr was insistent that apologetics cannot logically prove the truth of faith but it can confirm this truth by showing how it answers our deepest questions and yearnings. From my perspective apologetics does not so much confirm the truth of faith as the truth of faith confirms itself when it enters our experience convicting us of sin and bringing us assurance of salvation. The Spirit is, of course, free to use apologetic argumentation in support of the gospel, but Scripture tells us that His predilection is to reach out to people through the folly of the message of the cross.

* * * * * * * * * *

My doctoral thesis in its original form is only slightly different from this one. I have allowed the ideas and most of the nomenclature to stand. At the same time, I have tried to bring my thesis into line with contemporary English, which means among other things using gender inclusive people language. My motivation is not to bow to the demands of the feminists but to recognize that the usage of words shifts in a culture through the years, that words like "man" and "men" no longer include both sexes in the minds of a significant number of people. I have also made some other changes, mainly stylistic, but I have not altered my dissertation in order to bring it into conformity with my present-day views.

My position today on apologetics is remarkably similar to my position then, but I am now much more inclined to describe my theology as evangelical (a designation that I only rarely used at that time) rather than kerygmatic or apologetic.[4] The goal in an evangelical theology is not only the confession of faith in the gospel but also the conversion of the world to the gospel. I believe that both Niebuhr and Barth would not object strenuously to this spiritual vision. Niebuhr would probably say that our goal should be a just world rather than a Christianized world, which constitutes the millennial hope. Barth would strive for a society that allows for the freedom to proclaim the gospel as well as follow its mandates in political and social life. Both would vigorously oppose a theocracy in which the church relies on the state to enforce its moral prescriptions and ritual observances. I too reject a theocracy, but I am open to a Christocracy in which the rulers of this world are critiqued in light of a transcendent criterion that only faith has access to but that all people dimly know, yet truly experience at various times and places in their lives. This transcendent criterion is none other than the living Christ Himself, the Lord of all creation, sovereign over all nations, though this lordship is hidden from the mind of unbelieving humanity.

Donald G. Bloesch, 2002.

---

[4] See Donald G. Bloesch, *A Theology of Word & Spirit* (Downers Grove, IL: InterVarsity Press, 1992), pp. 212-49.

Prologue

Reinhold Niebuhr is indeed a prophetic voice on the American scene warning against a domesticated or culturized Christianity. What is not so well known is Niebuhr's venture into apologetics – seeking to establish the credibility of the faith in the public forum. My thesis is a modest attempt to throw light on this aspect of Niebuhr's theology.

I have chosen to analyze Niebuhr's apologetics for several reasons. First of all he wields a more powerful influence on the American theological scene than any other contemporary figure. His writings have also made a notable impact on the thinking of the world outside the church, at least in this country. Some secular philosophers after having encountered Niebuhr have been led to acknowledge the relevance of various Christian insights. Again, this theologian has delved into nearly every problem associated with the apologetic enterprise. He has given special attention to the epistemological problem – regarded by most theologians as basic to this enterprise. Finally, Niebuhr, on the basis of a critical analysis of the deeper meaning patterns within the Bible, has recognized how much the apologetics of the past has compromised the biblical message. He is acutely aware of the danger of syncretism, which is always present in the attempt to mediate between faith and culture, but he is also alert to the opposite danger of isolating faith from culture. He has sought to reevaluate the apologetic task in such a way as to make it consistent with the basic thrust of the Bible. In view of his concern to bring apologetics into line with biblical insights, I have addressed myself to this aspect of his theology. I have undertaken to show that Niebuhr's reevaluation does not do full justice to biblical revelation, especially where the nature of humanity is concerned. In order to bring the apologetic task into accord with biblical themes there is a pressing need for a more radical reappraisal of this task.

Chapter I

Introduction

Two Types of Theology

Before I begin my analysis of Reinhold Niebuhr's apologetic enterprise, it would be well to examine the two basic types of theological methodology – the apologetic and the kerygmatic.[1] These are ideal types[2] rather than concrete manifestations, synthetic constructs rather than empirical actualities. It would perhaps be more correct to assert that they signify emphases within various theological systems rather than theologies as such. On the other hand, I concur with several noted contemporary theologians that a typology such as this is of immense value in helping one to understand better certain basic divergences between theologians who have grappled with the difficult task of the communication of the gospel, especially to the world outside the church.[3] This typology is of particular importance to this thesis, since I intend to evaluate Niebuhr's apologetic approach in the light of a kerygmatic or confessional theology.

---

[1] This typology was enunciated by Paul Tillich in his *Systematic Theology* (Chicago: University of Chicago Press, 1951), 1:3-8.

[2] An "ideal type" as used by Max Weber and Ernst Troeltsch signifies a generalization that is never perfectly exemplified in any actual case. One arrives at an ideal type by selecting from empirical data comparable items and conceptualizing them with logical interrelatedness. The items are classified so as to exhaust alternative possibilities.

[3] Among theologians in our time who adhere to this or a similar typology are Karl Barth, Paul Tillich, Alan Miller, and H. Richard Niebuhr. Emil Brunner also might be listed, although he attempts to bridge the gulf between the two types. Reinhold Niebuhr does not deal with this typology explicitly, but he believes that it is legitimate. Many of his writings cannot be understood unless they are seen in the light of his attempt to counter a kerygmatic or Barthian methodology.

A theology might be regarded as apologetic if it attempts to answer attacks upon the faith from the outside world with the intention of persuading the world of the credibility of the faith. This answering is addressed not only to those outside the church but also to those inside the church primarily for the purpose of equipping them to meet secular attacks.[4] In its most advanced form apologetic theology is both a defensive and offensive enterprise in that it seeks not only to vindicate the faith against a hostile philosophy but also to overthrow or undermine the antagonist. Because apologetic theology prepares the Christian to converse with the outside world in defense of the faith, it seeks for common ground with the antagonist. Indeed, there can be no intelligible conversation apart from some common area of agreement. As Tillich says: "To be apologetic means to defend oneself in the face of an aggressor before a *mutually acknowledged criterion*"[5] (italics mine).

Apologetic theology finds the possibility of common ground between faith and unbelief in some doctrine of original revelation or common grace. The apologetic theologian, although he or she might acknowledge the corrupting power of sin, holds that there remains a point of connection between the human nous and divine logos, thereby making it possible for the natural person to respond to God as well as to seek God. Some types of apologetic theology emphasize this continuity between God and humanity more than others. The classical and also the Enlightenment apologists (both liberal and orthodox) went so far as to maintain that the Word of God is amenable to appropriation by human reason. Nearly every variation of apologetic theology views an apology as a potential means of grace, either as a means of preparatory (common) grace leading to the sermon or as a means of saving grace independent of

---

[4] Many apologists have drawn a technical distinction between apologetics and apology. Apologetics is addressed to Christians with the purpose of preparing them in the defense of the faith in general. An apology is directed to non-Christians; it meets a particular attack upon Christianity. In this thesis the term "apologetics" will for the most part include the connotations of "apology." The term "apologetic theology" refers to the general approach and methodology underlying every specific apologetics.

[5] Paul Tillich, *The Interpretation of History*, trans. N.A. Rasetzki and Elsa L. Talmey (New York: Charles Scribner's Sons, 1936), p. 42.

the sermon. It will be seen that the apologetics of Reinhold Niebuhr entails both the doctrine of common grace and the revelation in creation, which provide the necessary point of contact between reason and special revelation.

Kerygmatic or dogmatic theology, unlike apologetic theology, seeks neither to recommend nor to validate the faith; its sole aim is to confess the faith to the glory of God.[6] It does not set out to establish the credibility of the faith because it recognizes no common ground between God's Word and natural reason. It holds that because of our finitude as mortals we are unable to conceive of the unconditional God.[7] Because of our sin, we have been rendered incapable of seeking as well as responding to God. We can know God only when God breaks into our finite world and grants us the power to receive Him. Moreover, we are told that God has chosen to reveal Himself in this special way only through the heralding of the gospel (i.e., the "kerygma") as found in the Bible and the church. The kerygmatic theologian concentrates on explicating the Scriptural message not in order to convert the world but to please God, who alone can seal the kerygmatic truth in our hearts.

Kerygmatic theology, in contradistinction to apologetic theology, is oriented primarily about the sermon. Its purpose is to correlate the language of the church and the meaning of the gospel so that the gospel can be truly proclaimed not only to the church but

---

[6] Kerygmatic and dogmatic theology are not strictly synonymous. Dogmatics is technically the statement of the doctrinal tradition for the present situation. In some cases this statement has been grounded in a philosophical criterion rather than the Word of God in Scripture. It has been colored by an apologetic rather than a purely evangelistic concern. Kerygmatic theology (which is the bona fide dogmatic theology) makes revelation the sole basis for dogmatic formulation and witnessing its sole aim. Wherever "dogmatic theology" is referred to in this thesis it will be equated with or subsumed under "kerygmatic theology" unless otherwise stated. The term "confessional theology," despite its historic associations with Protestant scholastic theology, will also be regarded as identical with kerygmatic theology, unless otherwise stated. Because of the confusion that might ensue from these various terms, I shall use the term "kerygmatic theology" wherever possible.

[7] Kerygmatic theologians hold that original revelation does not sufficiently bridge the barrier of finitude because it has been shattered (although not necessarily destroyed) by sin. Common grace might well exist, but they believe that it does not really break the controlling power of sin and thereby enable the human subject to apprehend the gospel.

also to the world. Such an endeavor necessarily entails a study of the various interpretations of the gospel within the historic Christian community. Wrestling with interpretations that have been deemed heretical is the polemical side of kerygmatic theology. The task of explicating the Scriptural message also involves a scrutiny of the thinking of the world outside the church, since such thinking continually penetrates the sphere of theology, thereby providing the occasion for heresy.[8] Kerygmatic theologians acknowledge that within the church there is room for discussion and criticism. They believe, however, that in facing the world the church must confine itself to proclaiming the gospel, for the person of the world must first know the gospel before engaging in the task of critical understanding.[9] Kerygmatic theology strives to make possible the rendition of an intelligible sermon as over against an intelligible apology, for it holds that the sermon is the peculiar instrument of the Holy Spirit who alone builds the church and overcomes the world.

Although apologetic theology played no significant role in the New Testament period (which was dominated by kerygmatic theology), it emerged into prominence shortly thereafter. In the early church or patristic period the concern of most theologians was to validate the faith in the eyes of a hostile pagan world. Irenaeus and Tertullian to a lesser extent are notable exceptions in that they reacted vigorously against the apologetic enterprise.[10] Augustine

---

[8] The type of kerygmatic theology that I espouse entails an analysis of secular thought for the purpose not only of guarding against heresy but also of appropriating certain secular insights that have their source in common grace. See *infra*, pp. 124-126.

[9] According to Tillich, for kerygmatic theology "the 'situation' cannot be entered; no answer to the questions implied in it can be given .... The message must be thrown at those in the situation – thrown like a stone." *Systematic Theology* (Chicago: University of Chicago Press, 1951), 1:7.

[10] Irenaeus was especially critical of those who contended that the apostles "did ... frame their doctrine according to the capacity of their hearers, and gave answers after the opinions of their questioners." Irenaeus points out that Jesus never addressed his hearers, including his disciples, according to their pre-conceived notions. "He ... did not address them in accordance with their pristine notions, nor did He reply to them in harmony with the opinion of His questioners, but according to the doctrine leading to salvation, without hypocrisy or respect of person." Irenaeus, *Irenaeus Against Heresies* in Alexander Roberts and James Donaldson, ed. and trans., *The Ante-Nicene Fathers*, American edition (Grand Rapids, Michigan: Eerdmans, 1953), 1:418. Tertullian is less consistent in his stricture on apologetic theology, since he often attempts

tried to hold to both theological methods. He stressed the priority of faith over understanding; yet he believed that it was possible for an intelligible apology to prepare the way for faith.[11] In the medieval period the apologetic approach colored the whole theological enterprise, although apologetics was by no means the only theological discipline. In that medieval apologetics was directed primarily at groups that did not seriously threaten the hegemony of the church, it served practical purposes less than the reinforcement of the Christian consciousness.[12]

Apologetic theology has seen its greatest triumph in the modern period. Although kerygmatic theology was revivified in the Protestant Reformation, the theologians who followed the Reformers returned for the most part to the apologetic kind of thinking. This development was in one sense to be expected, since the post-Reformation period has witnessed the rise of a secular humanistic pattern of thought, which has penetrated every sphere of life. The seeds of revolt against biblical faith were already being planted in the early Renaissance period before the Reformation. This revolt was abetted by the rise of modern science symbolized by the Copernican and Darwinian revolutions, the new interest in the history of religions, the emergence of the higher criticism of the Bible, and the growth of nationalism, which all served in their own way to undermine the influence and authority of the church. Because Western culture has become increasingly alienated from the Christian mythos, the church has evermore concerned itself with the defense

---

to validate the truth of faith. His hostility towards apologetics can especially be seen in his *The Prescription Against Heretics*: "What indeed has Athens to do with Jerusalem? What concord is there between the Academy and the Church? what between heretics and Christians?... Away with all attempts to produce a mottled Christianity of Stoic, Platonic and dialectic composition! We want no curious disputation after possessing Christ Jesus, no inquisition after enjoying the gospel! With our faith, we desire no further belief." In Alexander Roberts and James Donaldson, ed., *The Ante-Nicene Fathers*, (Buffalo: Christian Literature Publishing Co., 1885), 3:246.

[11] The inconsistencies in Augustine's theology that have arisen partly because of his attempt to be both apologetic and kerygmatic (in the sense that I am using these terms) are admirably traced in Anders Nygren's *Agape and Eros*, trans. Philip S. Watson (Philadelphia: Westminster Press, 1953).

[12] See Hermann Schultz, *Outlines of Christian Apologetics*, trans. Alfred Bull Nichols (New York: Macmillan Co., 1905), pp. 8, 9.

both of the faith as a whole and of particular doctrines that have been singled out for attack by modernity.

In recent years apologetic theology in one or more of its various forms has come under severe criticism. One reason for this is the rise of philosophical skepticism (whether this be in the guise of logical positivism, historicism, or existentialism) which has cast doubt upon the possibility of rationally validating any given position. A second reason is the rediscovery of the Bible which was evidenced in Karl Barth's *Commentary On Romans* (first published in 1918). On the basis of a critical study of the Bible many theologians began to note the contradictions between much of the apologetic theology of the past and the message of the Bible. Although I shall speak of these two phenomena in the second chapter, especially as they concern Reinhold Niebuhr's theological enterprise, it would be well to mention a few contemporary figures who are responsible for the repudiation of the apologetics of the preceding centuries.

There are several theologians who have seriously questioned the whole apologetic enterprise as this has been traditionally understood. Karl Barth is perhaps the leading spokesman for this group. He holds that a theology that is biblically grounded must be dogmatic as opposed to apologetic. By this he means that the sole task of theology must be to explicate the dogmatic norm imbedded in the Bible rather than strive to validate the faith by appealing to secular norms. According to Barth the truth of faith cannot be related in any positive way to secular thought because sin has incapacitated the natural person not only from apprehending but also from seeking the gospel. We can know God only when the Spirit of God breaks into our disrupted world and transforms our inner being. Because the Spirit has chosen to act primarily through the message of the cross, it is up to people of faith to proclaim this message and let the gospel convert their hearers rather than trying to convert their hearers through their own power.[13] Barth's preference for the

---

[13] Reinhold Niebuhr succinctly paraphrases Barth's position: "One must not enter into a debate with modern culture to prove that its analysis of the plight of man is mistaken and that its proffered redemptions are illusory; one must preach the gospel and wait

kerygmatic as over against the apologetic method is especially evident in the following remarks.

> Because it is the Word of God, the revelation of God cannot be recommended and defended; it has no advocates and no propagandists. And, finally, one cannot profess one's belief in it by protesting and asserting that it exists. Revelation can only be believed in by becoming worthy of belief. Revelation can only be attested as any other unknown fact is attested by someone who happens to know it. Revelation can only be presupposed in our thinking and our speaking, and in our Christian theology and preaching too, in the way that certain axioms or objective facts are presupposed in every branch of knowledge, when the belief and the testimony and the presupposition are only forms of that one possible decision, the decision of obedience.[14]

H. Richard Niebuhr, who approaches the Barthian position on this point, also calls into question the underlying structure of the apologetic methodology. Drawing a distinction between apologetic and confessional methods, he tries to show that the former stands in contradiction to the basic insights of the Bible. He is convinced that the attempt to defend or justify the faith inevitably leads to the compromise and even to the dissolution of the faith. He supports this position by tracing the compromises of the faith in the theologies of Schleiermacher and Ritschl, both of which were dominated by the apologetic method. Niebuhr concludes: "Self-defense is the most prevalent source of error in all thinking and perhaps especially in theology and ethics."[15] And again:

> A critical historical theology cannot ... be an offensive or defensive enterprise which undertakes to prove the superiority of Christian faith to all other faiths; but it can be a

---

for the Holy Spirit to validate it." "An Answer to Karl Barth," *The Christian Century*, 66, no. 8 (Feb. 23, 1949), p. 234.

[14] Karl Barth, "The Christian Understanding of Revelation" in *Against the Stream* (London: SCM Press, 1954), p. 216. For a detailed analysis of apologetic theology see his *The Doctrine of the Word of God*, trans. G.T. Thomson (Edinburgh: T. & T. Clark, 1949), pp. 27-34; cf. pp. 392-399.

[15] H. Richard Niebuhr, *The Meaning of Revelation* (New York: Macmillan, 1941), p. viii.

confessional theology which carries on the work of self-criticism and self-knowledge in the church.[16]

There are many theologians today who severely censure modernism, that type of apologetic theology that tries to harmonize faith and secular thought; at the same time these scholars retain certain if not all of the underlying principles of the apologetic approach. In contradistinction to the Barthian school they believe in the possibility of common ground with secular thought, yet seek such ground only for the purpose of bringing people to a knowledge of the kerygma. These theologians take pains to differentiate their position from the Enlightenment theologies whose goal is to prove the content of faith. In the words of one of these theologians, Emil Brunner: "The God in whom we believe cannot be 'proved,' and the God who can be proved is not the God of faith."[17] Yet despite their belief that the truth of faith cannot be logically or scientifically demonstrated, they nevertheless concur that a certain type of apologetics can prepare the way for the acceptance of this truth. They are profoundly critical of those theologies that refuse to take seriously the limits of human reason. At the same time, they aver that there is an underlying continuity between the divine logos and the human nous, thereby making the apologetic enterprise possible. These theologians still see a place for apologetics, so long as it is rooted in the message of the Bible and not in any type of syncretism.

Reinhold Niebuhr is among those theologians who are intent on reevaluating rather than abandoning the apologetic task. Niebuhr is quick to reveal his uneasiness with medieval theology, especially Thomism, which he claims distorted certain revelatory insights within the Bible by too readily assimilating classical patterns of thought. He also inveighs against Protestant liberal theology, which he contends fused the truth of faith with the modern idea of progress. At the same time, Niebuhr will have nothing to do with

---

[16] *Ibid.*, pp. 17, 18.

[17] Emil Brunner, *The Christian Doctrine of God*, trans. Olive Wyon (Philadelphia: Westminster Press, 1950), p. 149.

those theologians who deny the validity of the apologetic task. He sternly rejects the radical Reformation theologies, including Barthianism, which he maintains isolate the truth of faith from all other truth, thereby making it irrelevant. He would seem to regard kerygmatic theology as a greater peril than liberal theology, at least for the present generation.

> The primary peril is that the wisdom of the Gospel is emptied of meaning by setting it into contradiction to the wisdom of the world and denying that the coherences and realms of meaning which the cultural disciplines rightfully analyze and establish have any relation to the Gospel.[18]

Reinhold Niebuhr is an apologetic theologian who is at the same time immersed in the biblical view of life. His primary concern is to lead the intelligentsia of his age to the gospel of Christ. He is not a preacher in the sense of an evangelist who simply heralds the message and calls his hearers to decision. Rather he is an apologist who attempts to analyze the self-understanding of the natural person and show how one is unable to understand oneself truly apart from revelation. Even his sermons are for the most part exercises in correlating the broken coherences of culture and the revelatory ground of all coherence rather than a straightforward explication of the biblical revelation. Whether Niebuhr does justice to the abiding insights of the Bible in his resolve to mediate between Christ and culture is the subject of this dissertation.

Statement of Thesis

It is my thesis that Niebuhr, despite his concern to bring apologetics into line with the biblical norm, diverges from this norm in several serious respects, particularly in his anthropology. And these deviations lead him to conceive of the apologetic task in a way which, in my judgment, cannot be justified on the basis of an appeal to the biblical witness. I contend that if we are to remain

---

[18] Reinhold Niebuhr, "Coherence, Incoherence, and Christian Faith" in his *Christian Realism and Political Problems* (New York: Charles Scribner's Sons, 1953), p. 192.

true to the biblical understanding the task of answering secular attacks upon the faith can be seriously entertained only when seen within the framework of a theology that seeks to proclaim rather than vindicate or recommend the Christian message, i.e., a theology that might be denominated as "kerygmatic" as over against "apologetic."

In chapter two I shall delve into Niebuhr's stricture against the dominant stream of traditional apologetics. I shall give particular attention to his criticisms of the biblical-classical synthesis and also of the theological synthesis with modern thought. It is significant that Niebuhr is much more sympathetic with the "eristical" apologetics of Pascal and Kierkegaard.[19] This is because Niebuhr himself utilizes this particular kind of apologetics in his effort to cope with the attacks of modern philosophy. Much of Niebuhr's criticism of the syncretistic type of apologetics is derived from his penetrating insight into the deeper meaning patterns of the Bible, which preclude any amalgamation of biblical and philosophical categories.

In chapter three I shall scrutinize Niebuhr's vindication of the apologetic principle, which might be defined as the possibility of common ground between faith and unbelief. Niebuhr finds this possibility in the concept of general or private revelation, which predicates a dialogue between the human spirit and the Eternal Spirit. Niebuhr is quick to point out, however, that this dialogue is partially broken by human sin. He criticizes the Roman Catholic interpretation of sin, which tends to minimize or even ignore its blinding power especially as this concerns the human apprehension of the moral law. At the same time, Niebuhr takes care to differentiate his position from that of Reformation and neo-Reformation theologies that tend to deny the fact that there is a dialogue between God and the human person. Niebuhr sides with Brunner over Barth in the debate on the "point of contact" between the gos-

---

[19] I have borrowed the term "eristical theology" from Emil Brunner. It signifies the method of undercutting the position of our adversary as over against the method of defense. Barth severely censures this method. See Barth, *The Doctrine of the Word of God*, pp. 28, 29.

pel and "the natural man." If there were no point of contact, according to Niebuhr, there would be no role for apologetics because apologetics is by its very nature an appeal to a criterion that connects the gospel and the structure of meaning held by our hearers.

Niebuhr sees apologetics as a means of validating the truth of faith (as we shall discern in chapter four). He lays particular emphasis on the negative validation of faith in which he tries to show how alternatives to Christian faith are either internally contradictory or else stand at variance with the brute facts of historical experience. Niebuhr also makes a place for a positive validation of faith, which consists in a correlation between the broken and limited apprehensions of culture and the ground of all apprehension, viz., Christ. It will be seen that this "correlation" is not nearly so obvious as that to which Tillich subscribes. Niebuhr sharply distinguishes his position from that of the more traditional apologists when he makes clear that his attempt to validate the faith does not necessarily prove it in the minds of our hearers. Niebuhr reveals his deep-seated biblical orientation when he insists that one cannot know the gospel of God except through repentance and decision. Yet he is convinced that although an intelligible apology cannot prove the truth of faith, it can demonstrate its relevance thereby making repentance and decision more likely. Again, in contradistinction to the classical apologists he takes care not to minimize the role of the Holy Spirit, but he implies that one channel of the Spirit's operation is an intelligible apology. In this chapter I shall try to compare Niebuhr's position with the positions of certain other eristical theologians as well as with two of the more kerygmatic theologians, Calvin and Barth.

In chapter five I shall subject Niebuhr's apologetic methodology to the scrutiny of the Bible. I shall first outline what I believe to be a genuinely biblical methodology. It will be seen that my conception of the authority and relevancy of the Bible is not too different from Niebuhr's. At the same time I shall undertake to point out certain basic differences. I shall endeavor to show that Niebuhr's contention that it is possible for the natural person to seek and respond to God cannot be supported by the testimony of Scripture, a testimony to which he himself adheres. I shall also try to show that the biblical testimony does not support Niebuhr's very broad interpretation of the means of grace.

In the final chapter I shall give my own reevaluation of the apologetic task.[20] In this endeavor I shall not hesitate to incorporate certain Niebuhrian insights that I believe to be genuinely biblical. My first aim will be to determine the mission or purpose of the church. I shall try to make clear that the mission of the church is to glorify God rather than to vindicate or prove God. The means whereby God is glorified is *witnessing* to His work of reconciliation on the cross. The primary task of theology is to enable the Christian to witness intelligibly in a concrete situation. Since it is the Holy Spirit who converts the minds of our hearers and since the Spirit has chosen to speak primarily through the "evangel" or the good news of God's revelation, theologians must expend their energies in explicating this good news. In so doing they dare not derive the content of their formulation from any source other than the revelation in the Bible. Their goal should be to correlate the language of the church with the meaning of Scripture rather than with the meaning-patterns of culture. I concur with H. Richard Niebuhr that theology is essentially a "confessional" enterprise.

Yet as genuine kerygmatic theologians we must recognize that the correlation of the language of the church with the meaning of Scripture entails much more than a knowledge of either historical theology or of Scripture. If we do not try to understand our faith in terms of the contemporary situation, we can neither witness intelligibly nor act responsibly. Both evangelism and social action presuppose "synoptic thinking" – the relating of the first principles of our faith to every area of our experience. But we cannot do this unless we are able to meet the attacks leveled upon the faith by secular philosophy. Reinhold Niebuhr as well as other apologists has been concerned with answering these attacks, and this remains a genuine theological concern, despite the asseverations of certain Barthians to the contrary.

---

[20] Niebuhr would very probably regard my attempt at reevaluating the apologetic task as a negation of this task. For my awareness of the ambiguity caused by my retention of the term "apologetics" see *infra*, pp. 124-126.

One of the basic problems involved in the task of faith seeking understanding is the relation between revelation and reason. I contend that although sin shatters the continuity between the divine logos and the human nous, the basic ontological relation remains intact. The "imago Dei" has been obfuscated, but it still exists. Despite this fact, there can be no common area of understanding between God and humanity because the human will is in bondage to the driving force of sin. There can be no possibility of viable connection between the coherences of the gospel and the coherences of reason because the latter are oriented about the idolatrous self rather than God. Nevertheless, through the power of the Holy Spirit the elected person's reason is momentarily liberated from its idolatrous orientation and is thereby enabled to apprehend the truth of faith as well as relate this truth to all areas of experience. Against Niebuhr I maintain that there is no power inherent in humanity that can serve as a basis for knowing God's Word, but such a power is bestowed on the elected person by the Holy Spirit in the event of preaching. We can know God's Word because a point of contact with the Word is created within us by the Holy Spirit as the Spirit acts through the proclaimed and written Gospel. Although my theological orientation is decidedly kerygmatic as opposed to apologetic, at the same time I take exception to certain extreme theological positions that might also be termed kerygmatic and yet that tend to deny or obscure the role of "sanctified reason" – reason grounded in faith.

In the concluding section I shall try to show that a certain kind of apologetics is necessary not as an introduction to the sermon but as a supplementation. Apologetics must equip theologians to answer attacks upon the faith not for the purpose of validating the faith (as Niebuhr says), but rather in order to amplify or illumine the faith. This "transformed apologetics" has for its aim "faith seeking understanding" rather than the persuasion or conversion of the unbeliever. It is envisaged in the final analysis not in terms of a conversation with the world but in terms of a conversation within the church for the purpose of helping Christians to integrate their faith and experience. At the same time, it has an indirect bearing on the communication of the faith to the world in that it is a necessary precondition of intelligible witnessing (which remains the dominant concern of the church). While there is still a role for a certain kind of "apologetical" work (although Niebuhr would call this by a different name), this work must be brought into the service of witnessing rather than apological conversation as this has been traditionally understood. The place for an apologetics that is oriented about revelation rather than a criterion held in common with secular thought is within the context of a kerygmatic theology.

Chapter II

Niebuhr's Break with Traditional Apologetics

Background of Niebuhr's Polemic

In order to appreciate Niebuhr's polemic against the dominant stream of traditional apologetics, one must know something of the source of his concerns. Two key factors that have contributed to Niebuhr's break with the older theologies are his participation in the revival of biblical theology and his encounter with contemporary forms of philosophical skepticism.

Niebuhr's steadily more conservative approach to the Bible through the years might be regarded in one sense as a spiritual pilgrimage. In his earlier works he very seldom alludes to the biblical norm or the biblical message. He holds that the goal of human action in religion is to revere personality (rather than to witness to the biblical revelation).[1] Instead of a biblical perspective, he speaks of an "ideal perspective."[2] Instead of vindicating the biblical revelation, he upholds "religion" or the "religious view of life." His theology is oriented more about the values of our religious heritage than God's decisive action in the history mirrored in the Bible. Yet even in his earliest writings Niebuhr reveals an abiding reverence for the sacred writings that constitute the Bible and an earnest concern to grapple with the thorny problem of the authority of the Bible for our age. In his attempt to formulate a position on this question, he was compelled to break with the liberal position on biblical author-

---

[1] Reinhold Niebuhr, *Does Civilization Need Religion?* (New York: Macmillan, 1927), p. 79.

[2] *Ibid.*, p. 164.

ity in which the Bible is a norm for value judgments and embrace a neo-orthodox position in which the Bible is a testimony to revelation.[3] He was aided in this transition by the renewal of interest in the message of the Bible that characterizes so much of contemporary theology.

In his theological maturity Niebuhr regards the Bible as a record as well as a medium of God's disclosure of His will and purpose. The center of the Bible is the "kerygma," i.e., the story of what God has done for us in the person of Jesus Christ.[4] The "kerygma" for Niebuhr as well as for many other biblical theologians is not only God's decisive act in history but also the apostolic apprehension or interpretation of this act.[5] Niebuhr for the most part makes this interpretation the criterion of his scrutiny of the biblical record. At the same time, in his search for a standard that eludes historical contingency he sometimes makes his ultimate criterion "agape" or the "mind of Christ." Niebuhr seems to vacillate between the apostolic interpretation of the gospel, which can be stated in terms of propositions, and the "law of love," which eludes rational definition.

Niebuhr's principal divergence from fundamentalism lies in his adamant refusal to take literally what the Bible says regarding God's decisive acts. Having been fully immersed in the higher criticism of the Bible he has been made poignantly aware that the natural or original meaning of the biblical text is often different from its literal meaning. According to Niebuhr whenever the biblical witnesses tried to depict the mysterious action of God in history, they were compelled to employ myth as opposed to literal language. By myth Niebuhr means an imaginative and dramatic depiction of "some meaning or reality, which is not subject to exact analysis but

---

[3] Reinhold Niebuhr, *Human Nature* in *The Nature and Destiny of Man* (New York: Charles Scribner's Sons, 1951), pp. 136-7.

[4] Reinhold Niebuhr, *Faith and History* (New York: Charles Scribner's Sons, 1949), p. 141.

[5] Cf. *Ibid.*, p. 141; "Coherence, Incoherence, and Christian Faith" in *Christian Realism and Political Problems* (New York: Charles Scribner's Sons, 1953),p. 200.

can nevertheless be verified in experience."[6] He takes care to differentiate what he regards as the biblical myths from the "pre-scientific myths," which occupy Bultmann's attention. These latter myths "disregard what may have always been known, or have now become known, about the ordered course of events in the world."[7] The myths concerning the creation, fall, incarnation, and second coming are permanent myths in that they describe events that elude the temporal or causal sequence and therefore cannot be subsumed under scientific or rationally determinate categories. Niebuhr acknowledges that there are also pre-scientific myths or fragments of such myths in the Bible. He supports Bultmann's contention that the message of the Bible must be cleansed of these particular myths, but he faults Bultmann for not making a sufficiently sharp distinction between the various kinds of myths and thereby undermining the truth embodied in the kerygma.[8] Niebuhr is rigorously insistent that myth is an essential part of the language of revelation, because he finds this to be the key to the uniqueness of the biblical faith.[9]

On the basis of an encounter with the mind of God as revealed in the Bible, Niebuhr has become sharply critical of any kind of fusion between biblical faith and ontological speculation. He has become keenly aware of certain basic tensions between what he terms the "biblical" or "Hebraic" view of life and the ontological or "Hellenic" view. It would be well to enumerate some of these tensions (as Niebuhr understands them). Whereas the Bible presupposes a radical discontinuity between God and humanity, which is bridged only by a divine-human encounter, ontology (whether in its Greek or modern forms) is grounded in an immanental view, which tends to identify God with what is deepest within the self or the world. Whereas the Bible speaks of God as the "Other" who stands over against humanity, ontology equates God with the "depth of reason" or the "ground of being." Whereas the Bible re-

---

[6] Reinhold Niebuhr, *The Self and the Dramas of History* (New York: Charles Scribner's Sons, 1955), p. 97.

[7] *Ibid.*

[8] *Ibid.*

[9] For a critical analysis of Niebuhr's conception of myth see *infra*, pp. 86-87.

gards our knowledge of God as necessarily broken and limited since it has its source in discontinuous moments of encounter, ontology presupposes that it is possible to arrive at an ultimate and universal picture of God. Whereas the Bible regards God as a free Being who stands over against the categories of reason, ontology regards God as the supreme case among the categories. In the Bible God is depicted as particular and concrete; ontology invariably equates God with that which is most abstract and universal. Whereas the Bible utilizes mythical and paradoxical language to describe the mysterious activity of God, ontology favors univocal and strictly logical language. The Bible speaks of sin in terms of wilful rebellion; ontology links sin with finitude and ignorance. Although Niebuhr vigorously opposes any fusion between the Hebraic and Hellenic views, he nevertheless appreciates some of the insights of the ontologists and implies that the Hebraic needs to be supplemented by the Hellenic view.[10]

Among the skeptical philosophies that Niebuhr avails himself of in his polemic against ontology is Kantianism. Immanuel Kant was not a bona fide skeptic in that he acknowledged the validity of mathematical and scientific knowledge. In his *Critique of Pure Reason* he argues against Hume that these types of knowledge are universal and necessary because the apriori forms of our sensibility and understanding structure all objects of possible experience.[11] Yet Kant goes on to maintain that such knowledge does not apply to the "thing in itself," for this would make the ultimate reality dependent upon the structure of the mind. The mind is competent in the phenomenal realm, but it cannot penetrate the noumenal or metaphysical realm. In his subsequent critiques Kant attempts to bridge the gulf between the noumenal and phenomenal realms by means of moral and aesthetic intuition. Yet he is always quick to point out that such intuition yields only practical insight, not theoretical knowledge. Although Niebuhr seldom refers to Kant, it can

---

[10] *The Self and the Dramas of History*, p. 77.

[11] Immanuel Kant, *Critique of Pure Reason*, trans. J.M.D. Meiklejohn, revised ed. (New York: Willey Book Co., 1943).

be shown that he accepts much of the Kantian framework. Like Kant he acknowledges the reliability of mathematical and scientific knowledge, but again like Kant he is skeptical concerning human ability to penetrate the realm of the unconditional and absolute.

Niebuhr also leans heavily on a type of contemporary skepticism known as historicism. It is well to note the critical role of Kant in the development of this philosophy. Since Kant's view served to produce an hiatus between spirit and nature, it made possible the independent development of the sciences of the spirit (the "*Geisteswissenschaften*"). Unlike the natural sciences the social (or spiritual) sciences emphasize not universal laws but individuality and development. Dilthey, who was among the first to discuss the methodology of the social sciences, contended that we cannot understand a person's behavior except in terms of the meaning-patterns of the culture in which that person lives. Because one's ideas are shaped and colored by one's cultural matrix (which is unlike other cultural matrices and which is always in the process of development), no judgment can be regarded as absolute (not even that of the social scientist). Just as Kant emphasized the structural limitations of reason, so Dilthey stressed its historical limitations. This is what many philosophers call historicism or historical relativism; it also might be termed cultural determinism. In one form or another it has enlisted the support of such seminal thinkers as Karl Marx, Karl Mannheim, Ernst Troeltsch, Charles Sumner, Oswald Spengler, and Pitirim Sorokin.

Niebuhr utilizes historicism in his critique of any system that claims that it is possible to achieve perfection, whether this be in terms of virtue or truth.

> There can be nothing absolute in history, no matter how frequently God may intervene in it. Man cannot live without a sense of the absolute, but neither can he achieve the absolute. He may resolve the tragic character of that fact by religious faith, by the experience of grace in which the unattainable is experienced in anticipatory terms, but he can

never resolve in purely ethical terms the conflict between what is and what ought to be.[12]

He particularly appeals to Marxism in his attempt to counter ontological speculation in theology. In Marxist thinking a theology or philosophy can be shown to be nothing more than an "ideology," i.e., an attempt to rationalize economic self-interest. Niebuhr acknowledges what he calls an "ideological taint" in all human reasoning: "Complete rational objectivity in a social situation is impossible."[13] For "our mind is never a pure and abstract intelligence when it functions amidst the complexities of human relations. There is no vantage point, individual or collective, in human history from which we could judge its movements with complete impartiality."[14] Even the theologian is subject to the ideological taint and therefore cannot claim to possess unconditional truth when arguing with an unbeliever. It must be recognized that Niebuhr's interpretation of the ideological taint is much more radical than Marx's. Marx exempted the proletarian class from his stricture; all classes and peoples fall under Niebuhr's stricture. Moreover, Marx regards "dishonest rationalizations as primarily due to the finiteness of human perspectives."[15] Niebuhr sees in ideology an element of wilful dishonesty which is not necessitated by our finitude.[16] While Marx locates the root of ideology in economic interest, Niebuhr sees its source in the rebellious human will.

Niebuhr also assimilates various insights of Sigmund Freud in the endeavor to safeguard and vindicate the truth of the kerygma. Just as the historical relativists stress the conditioning power of a person's external environment, so Freud stresses the conditioning influence of the internal environment. According to Freud the rea-

---

[12] Reinhold Niebuhr, "Must We Do Nothing?" *The Christian Century*, 49, no. 13 (March 30, 1932), p. 417.

[13] Reinhold Niebuhr, *Moral Man and Immoral Society* (New York: Charles Scribner's Sons, 1932), p. xiv.

[14] Reinhold Niebuhr, *Discerning the Signs of the Times* (New York: Charles Scribner's Sons, 1946), p. 8.

[15] *Ibid.*, p. 10.

[16] *Ibid.* Cf. *Human Nature*, pp. 46-48.

soning process is very much determined by the vital impulses (the "id"), which are predominantly of a sexual nature. Niebuhr has some very cogent criticisms of Freud's philosophy, but he accepts Freud's indictment of "reason's pretended mastery over vital impulse."[17]

Moreover, Niebuhr endorses many of the insights of existentialism, a philosophy that holds that the path to knowledge lies in personal involvement and decision. This school of thought stems from Kierkegaard, but many of Kierkegaard's categories are Kantian, and some of his basic insights are anticipated in Kant's *Critique of Practical Reason*. A guiding principle of existentialist philosophy is that one cannot understand unless one has already committed oneself. This principle is evident in Niebuhr's contention that a person must first believe before being able to understand the truth of faith. Moreover, Niebuhr holds that this truth is not some abstraction that can be apprehended merely by reason; it must "be apprehended by man in the total unity of his personality."[18] He reproves those apologists who would treat the truth of faith from the standpoint of a spectator or disinterested observer. According to Niebuhr this truth can be perceived only by one who participates in it, only by one who has decided for it at great risks.

Niebuhr draws on the insights of the various forms of philosophical skepticism in order to undercut the synthesis of biblical faith and ontology, whether this be in the guise of mysticism, idealism, or naturalism. From his perspective the truth of faith cannot be amalgamated with ontology because it is impossible to subsume the living Word of God under a conditioned structure of meaning. Even a theology that strives to free itself from ontology cannot contain the Word of God, for it also is infected by the ideological taint. A theology can at the most acknowledge that its insights into the meaning of the Word are broken and limited (although they might be valid) and that they await their fulfillment at the end of history when faith shall be transmuted into sight.

---

[17] *Human Nature*, p. 36.
[18] *Faith and History*, p. 141.

Analysis of Syncretic Theology

Even in his earliest writings Niebuhr warns against the biblical-classical synthesis, although he suggests that this synthesis was inevitable. He writes of the early period of Christianity:

> Naïve Christianity was unable to maintain itself in the Graeco-Roman world without making concessions to its intellectual scruples and paying for its conquests by incorporating Hellenic philosophies in its theology. The gospel was diluted with neo-Platonism to make it more palatable for a cultured world. The naively and dramatically conceived omnipotence of God was metaphysically elaborated and inevitably betrayed the church into an essential pantheism.[19]

Niebuhr is sharply critical of the synthesis with classical philosophy in both its Catholic and liberal forms. I shall first delve into Niebuhr's evaluation of Roman Catholicism, giving special attention to his criticisms of the Catholic doctrines of revelation and the church.

Niebuhr holds that by blurring the radical discontinuity between revelatory and strictly determinate knowledge, Catholicism tended to subvert the meaning of revelation. In the Bible revelation is conceived in terms of personal encounter rather than of doctrine. Since this encounter involves an encounter of minds, knowledge is revealed, but this knowledge can never be fully grasped or objectified and must be unveiled ever again. Niebuhr believes that this biblical insight was obscured by the early apologists and also the medieval theologians. Nearly all of them held to some form of propositional revelation. What is revealed is a truth that is accessible to reason and, in the thinking of some scholars, this truth completes reason. The radical difference between God's word and human reason was lost sight of completely in many circles.[20] Rather than util-

---

[19] *Does Civilization Need Religion?* p. 201.

[20] Harnack, whose views on the Catholic synthesis closely parallel those of Niebuhr, maintains that according to the apologists "grace can be nothing else than the stimulation of the powers of reason existent in man; revelation is supernatural only in re-

izing paradox and myth in describing God's self-disclosure in the Bible, the scholastic theologians sought to incorporate this event into a logically coherent system. Niebuhr cites the scholastic doctrine of the two natures of Christ as an example of a tendency "to reduce Christian faith to metaphysical truths which need not be apprehended inwardly by faith."[21]

According to Niebuhr the synthesis with ontology has led to the compromise of the biblical understanding not only of special revelation but also of the revelation in creation. Whereas the apostles held that human insights into this revelation are partial and broken because of sin, Catholic theology finds in this revelation universal rational norms upon which it constructs an elaborate theory of natural law. Niebuhr argues that by making these norms too neat and rigid, Catholicism not only betrays biblical insights regarding the blinding power of sin but also is unable "to give adequate moral guidance to men in the unique occasions of history and under the shifting circumstances of historical development."[22] Niebuhr avers that the idea of natural law is not derived from the Bible at all but rather from Stoicism.[23] He maintains that the Catholic doctrine of natural law "clearly substitutes rational ontology for the biblical dramatic apprehension of the meaning of history."[24]

Niebuhr also has problems with the ecclesiology of Catholicism. Indeed, the perversion of the meaning of the church followed the perversion of the meaning of revelation. By conceiving of revelation as a body of truth accessible to reason, the church came to regard revelation as something that it possessed. It was only a short step for the church to assume the roles of the guardian and the dispenser of divine truth and power. From a charismatic fellowship governed only the Holy Ghost, the church became an hierarchical

---

spect of its form." Adolf von Harnack, *History of Dogma*, trans. from 3rd German edition by Neil Buchanan (Boston: Roberts Brothers, 1897), 1:225.

[21] Reinhold Niebuhr, *Human Destiny* in *The Nature and Destiny of Man*, p. 61.

[22] *The Self and the Dramas of History*, p. 102.

[23] Reinhold Niebuhr, "Love and Law in Protestantism and Catholicism" in *Christian Realism and Political Problems*, p. 157.

[24] *The Self and the Dramas of History*, p. 102.

institution centered in Rome and governed by a pope who was believed to possess the keys to heaven. Niebuhr holds that Augustine did much to accelerate this idolatrous tendency by blurring the lines between the church and the kingdom of God.[25] Niebuhr points out that by the time of Thomas Aquinas the church was more closely correlated with both the kingdom of Christ and the body of Christ. One consequence of this aggrandizement of the institutional church was "to reduce 'grace' in the religious life to a power which could be magically transmitted."[26]

Moreover, Niebuhr argues that Roman Catholic Christianity tends to downplay the historical significance of the faith. Much of this argument is related to his criticisms of the Catholic doctrines of revelation and the church (as we shall see). By portraying God as the *potestas absoluta* (absolute power) rather than the Living Lord of history, Catholicism deemphasizes the mighty deeds of God as recorded in the Bible.[27] By conceiving of revelation for the most part in terms of revealed propositions rather than of divinely illuminated

---

[25] According to Niebuhr Augustine confused the church with the kingdom of God by regarding the church "as the only society in which perfect justice prevails." *Faith and History*, p. 201. Niebuhr is for the most part very appreciative of Augustine. He contends that Augustine on the whole had a much more acute understanding of the tensions within the Christian faith than most other theologians, both medieval and modern, even though he did not sufficiently apprehend the paradox of grace and sin within the life of the Christian. Niebuhr says: "Whatever the defects of the Augustine approach may be, we must acknowledge his immense superiority both over those who preceded him and those who came after him. A part of that superiority was due to his reliance upon biblical rather than idealistic or naturalistic conceptions of selfhood. But that could not have been the only cause, else Christian systems before and after him would not have been so inferior. Or were they inferior either because they subordinated the biblical-dramatic conception of human selfhood too much to the rationalistic scheme, as was the case with medieval Christianity culminating in the thought of Thomas Aquinas? or because they did not understand that the corruption of human freedom could not destroy the original dignity of man, as was the case with the Reformation with its doctrines of sin, bordering on total depravity and resulting in Luther's too pessimistic approach to political problems?" "Augustine's Political Realism" in *Christian Realism and Political Problems*, pp. 145, 146.

[26] *The Self and the Dramas of History*, p. 103.

[27] "When Hellenic concepts of 'being' are substituted for the idea of a 'creator,' and of the mystery of creation as the ontological anchor for the historic revelation, the emphasis is invariably shifted from the content of the revelation, which is, according to the Bible, the reconciliation between God and man on the divine initiative. The 'Incarnation' becomes instead the revelation of the eternal in the temporal and the dramatic account of the reconciliation between God and man is obscured." *Ibid.*, pp. 98-99.

events, it tends to make the object of faith a doctrine rather than a divine act. By depicting our hope so often in terms of individual transformation and union with the Eternal (cf. Plotinus), it diverts attention from the consummation of history in the second coming of Christ. The doctrine of the church as the "continuing incarnation" also serves to cloud the historical decisiveness of biblical revelation. It is not the sacrifice of Christ on the cross that is the focal point in Catholic theology but rather the re-creation of this sacrifice in the mass. It is not what God has done for us in the history mirrored in the Bible; it is what God through the church confers upon us now that is regarded as decisive for our salvation. Niebuhr holds that by too closely identifying the kingdom of Christ with a static hierarchical institution, Roman Catholic theology has served to dissipate the dynamic-historic strand in the Christian faith.

It can be shown that Niebuhr believes that the biblical-classical synthesis as it is found in Roman Catholic theology has distorted nearly every major doctrine of Christian faith. Besides those that I have treated, I could mention the doctrines of the Holy Spirit, the sovereignty of God, grace, love, and sin. It will not be necessary to trace the distortion in every one of these doctrines. One can infer its nature from what has already been said regarding Niebuhr's criticisms of the Catholic synthesis. The compromise of the biblical view of sin within Catholic theology will be treated in some detail in chapter three.

Niebuhr has been no less outspoken in his indictment of Protestant liberal theology. Here again he finds the defect in a synthesis of biblical motifs and ontology. The ontology that he deals with in this connection has a modern as over against a classical predilection, although its origins are partly classical. The specific emphasis of modern ontology is on growth and creativity.[28] This

---

[28] Niebuhr differentiates the classical and modern views in the following manner: "The ascription of historical evil to the natural or the primitive gives modern culture its common ground with classical thought. But it has a radically different scheme of redemption from the inertia of nature. It believes that history redeems man from nature. The same history which classical culture equates with the cycles of growth and decay in nature is regarded by modern culture as a realm of indeterminate growth. It has this confidence, even though it does not distinguish history too sharply from nature, since

emphasis is partially derived from the scientific analyses of the structure of the world, particularly the organic world. Niebuhr criticizes liberal theologians for seeking to amalgamate the faith and a philosophy grounded upon the processes of nature as revealed by science:

> When religious apologists found it necessary to readjust the age-old affirmations of faith to the evolutionary facts revealed by science they usually sank even more deeply into the morass of pantheistic and monistic philosophy. The old and naïve conceptions of a capricious omnipotence working its will upon natural phenomena became manifestly untenable and a way had to be found to relate divine purpose to and discover the area of creativity in the natural and cosmic processes. It was practically inevitable that such a task would be accomplished only by an overemphasis on divine immanence and a consequent betrayal of religion into a sentimental optimism.[29]

In Niebuhr's opinion the fusion of faith with modern ontology has resulted in the compromise of the faith at several different levels. Rather than upholding the uniqueness of the biblical revelation, liberal theologians subordinated revelation under the general category of religion.[30] Rather than exalting God as the creator, they made God contingent upon the immanent process. Rather than heralding the biblical message of a kingdom beyond history, they identified the kingdom with "that ideal society which modern culture hoped to realize through the evolutionary process."[31] Whereas the New Testament tells us to base our hope on the Lord of history, the liberals placed their hope in the historic process itself. They very

---

nature is also discovered to be in the process of growth. It is growth, therefore, which is the meaning of life and the guarantee of the fulfillment of its true meaning." *Faith and History*, p. 68.

[29] *Does Civilization Need Religion?* pp. 204-205.

[30] It must be borne in mind that when Niebuhr speaks of "liberal theology" as well as of other theological types, he has in mind ideal types rather than concrete systems. He very seldom differentiates the various strands within the theological types, and this perhaps might be regarded as one of his failings.

[31] Reinhold Niebuhr, *An Interpretation of Christian Ethics* (New York: Harper & Brothers, 1935), p. 15.

seldom spoke of Christ as God Incarnate but more often as "the good man of Galilee, symbol of human goodness and human possibilities without suggestion of the limits of the human and the temporal – in short, without the suggestion of transcendence."[32] Liberal theology interpreted the Christian love commandment as demanding that we love our fellowman not because God loves us (as Scripture says), but because "we ought to have 'respect for personality.'"[33] The biblical conception of sin "was translated into the imperfections of ignorance, which an adequate pedagogy would soon overcome."[34]

Niebuhr finds the root of the modern heresy in a lack of appreciation for the basic discontinuity between God and nature. This discontinuity arises not only from the fact that God is unconditional and the human world is conditioned, but also because God is holy and the human world is tainted by sin. The God of the Bible, according to Niebuhr, cannot be located in the depth of the self or of nature, since God transcends the processes of nature and history. "It is by faith in transcendence that a profound religion is saved from complete capitulation to the culture of any age, past or present."[35] Apart from such a faith religion degenerates into relativism and even nihilism.[36]

---

[32] *Ibid.*

[33] *Ibid.*, p. 213.

[34] *Ibid.*, p. 15.

[35] *Ibid.*, p. 16.

[36] Niebuhr acutely traces the relativistic propensity in the religion of the Romantics: "The religious relativism of the romantics reveals how far they have departed from the Christian faith. In Christianity the unique individual finds the contingent and arbitrary aspect of his existence tolerable because it is related to, judged and redeemed by the eternal God, who transcends both the rational structure and the arbitrary facts of existence in the universe. In romantic religion the unique and arbitrary character of existence does not find its limit and fulfillment in an eternal world of meaning but expresses itself in terms of limitless pretension. 'Every man,' said Lavater, 'has his own religion just as he has his own face and every one has his own God just as he has his own individuality.' While Schleiermacher does not follow this position through to such an explicit polytheism, he thinks in the same terms. 'If you want to grasp the idea of religion as a factor in the infinite and progressive development of the World Spirit then you must give us the vain and empty desire for one religion,' he declares. This means that the only meaning of life is that there should be a variety of meaning. This untenable position, beginning in relativism, ends in nihilism." *Human Nature*, p. 86.

Niebuhr opposes a synthesis not only with the so-called modern ontology, but also with more recent types of philosophical speculation. Although appreciating the insights of existentialism, he is wary of any synthesis with this philosophy. Niebuhr holds that existentialism makes passionate subjectivity rather than revelation the criterion of truth. He contends that with such an epistemological criterion, one is rendered incapable of combating a false religion that embodies passion and subjectivity.[37] He also concludes that existentialist philosophy, especially in its contemporary forms, "while understanding the unique freedom of man, is more intent to assert it in defiance of death than to acknowledge that it is subject to corruption."[38] It does not see that we need to be saved from sin rather than from death. Niebuhr is unhappy with Bultmann's theology on the grounds that it fuses the truth of the kerygma and existentialism.[39]

It is interesting to note Niebuhr's criticisms of Tillich. Tillich, like Niebuhr, is intent on reevaluating the apologetic task in the light of the insights of the Bible. Tillich espouses a method of correlation by which theology attempts to answer the questions of philosophy and contrasts this with the older apologetic method of synthesis. Niebuhr holds that Tillich does not succeed in avoiding a synthesis with ontology, specifically the ontology of the classical type.[40] In an essay in the symposium on Tillich, Niebuhr complains that Tillich too closely links sin with finitude, thereby subjecting humanity to an "ontological necessity."[41] In his recent book *The Self and the Dramas of History* Niebuhr avers that knowledge of

---

[37] "Coherence, Incoherence, and Christian Faith" in *Christian Realism and Political Problems*, pp. 192-3.

[38] *The Self and the Dramas of History*, p. 97.

[39] *Ibid*.

[40] When Tillich first came to America it appeared that there was considerable affinity between his theology and Niebuhr's. Niebuhr stated this affinity in his article "The Contribution of Paul Tillich", *Religion in Life*, 6, no. 4 (Autumn, 1937), pp. 574-581. Since then, however, the two theologians have been going in very different directions.

[41] See Reinhold Niebuhr, "Biblical Thought and Ontological Speculation in Tillich's Theology" in *The Theology of Paul Tillich*, ed. Charles W. Kegley & Robert W. Bretall (New York: Macmillan, 1952), pp. 216-227.

God is dialogic – having its source in a divine-human encounter – rather than unitive – conceived in terms of union with the ground of being. Niebuhr does not mention Tillich by name in this book, but it is generally agreed that this book is directed in part against Tillich's ontological synthesis.[42]

Niebuhr sharply criticizes the syncretic forms of apologetics on the grounds that they strive to contain the truth of faith within a rational synthesis. By trying to fit the faith into a structural mold, the apologists in reality are subordinating faith to reason and are thereby making reason into a god.

> Though the religious faith through which God is apprehended cannot be in contradiction to reason in the sense that the ultimate principle of meaning cannot be in contradiction to the subordinate principle of meaning which is found in rational coherence yet, on the other hand religious faith cannot be simply subordinated to reason or made to stand under its judgment. When this is done the reason which asks the question whether the God of religious faith is plausible has already implied a negative answer in the question because it has made itself God and naturally cannot tolerate another.[43]

---

[42] For a cogent comparison of the theologies of Niebuhr and Tillich in the light of Niebuhr's recent book see Will Herberg, "The Three Dialogues of Man," *The New Republic*, 132 (May 16, 1955), pp. 28-31. For a further elucidation of the differences between Tillich and Niebuhr see Tillich's criticism of Niebuhr and Niebuhr's reply in *Reinhold Niebuhr: His Religious, Social and Political Thought*, ed. Charles W. Kegley and Robert W. Bretall (New York: Macmillan, 1956), pp. 36-43; 432-433.

[43] *Human Nature*, pp. 165-166.

Attitude Towards Other Kinds of Apologetics

Although Niebuhr is extremely critical of modernism, that type of theology that fuses faith and culture, it might be well to peruse his analysis of other kinds of apologetic theology.

Since I have said nothing concerning his attitude towards the classical proofs for the existence of God (both ontological and cosmological), I shall briefly mention it here. Niebuhr nowhere gives an extensive analysis of these proofs, but from what he says we can safely assume that he considers them as only another variation of the merging of the truth of faith with ontology. For Niebuhr the God whose existence can be logically demonstrated is not the God of faith, but an abstraction or idea.

What about Niebuhr's attitude towards the various types of apologetics based upon miracles and biblical prophecy? Niebuhr will have nothing to do with any approach that isolates the truth of faith from other truth by an appeal to miracles. For him the miracles of the Bible as well as the inner meaning of the prophecies can be appreciated only with the eyes of faith. They are not to be regarded as signs or proofs of the truth of faith. Niebuhr has no sympathy with those theologians who attempt to build their system upon miraculous facts .

> Error arises when the effort is made to guard the uniqueness of the truth of faith and to prevent its absorption into a general system of knowledge by insisting that Christian truth is miraculously validated and has no relation to any truth otherwise known. This is the error to which Protestant literalism is particularly prone. Its consequence is cultural obscurantism. The truth of faith, thus jealously guarded, degenerates into a miraculous historical fact. Miracles may be believed without the repentance which is the prerequisite of the renewal of life. The tendency to transmute a truth of faith, which can be known only by a person in the totality and wholeness of his life, into a miraculous fact, which the credulous but not the sophisticated may easily believe, ac-

counts for the frequent spiritual aridity of Protestant orthodoxy.[44]

Niebuhr takes a negative position with regard to the miracle proofs primarily on biblical grounds. First of all he contends that a "fact" of history, attested by a miracle, can be known apart from any subjective commitment. But the Bible tells us that the truth of the gospel is apprehended only through repentance and decision. Moreover, Niebuhr argues that his position is "in accord with Christ's own rejection of signs and wonders as validations of his messianic mission."[45]

Within the framework of Niebuhr's theology it would be possible to hold that the apologetics based on miracles is only another variation of the synthesis with ontological speculation.[46] Since a miracle is none other than a proposition regarding a supernatural occurrence, it can be subsumed within a logically coherent system. Even though the miracle might be the key principle within the system, it nevertheless remains a principle amenable to rational appropriation and not a truth that stands over against the pattern of rational coherence. Like the principles of a purely natural theology, it can be appropriated apart from repentance and faith.

Although Niebuhr is extremely critical of much of the apologetic theology of the past, he does uphold one type of apologetics – what I have called "eristics." This type of apologetics was exemplified in the theologies of Pascal and Kierkegaard. It is currently advocated in various degrees by such theologians as Brunner, Richardson, and Tillich. Eristics consists in the attempt to undercut philosophical speculation and show where reason points beyond

---

[44] *Faith and History*, p. 166. For Niebuhr's criticisms of Lutheran orthodoxy see his article "The Heresy Trials", *Christianity and Crisis*, 15, no. 22 (Dec. 26, 1955), pp. 171-172.

[45] "Coherence, Incoherence, and Christian Faith" in *Christian Realism and Political Problems*, p. 198.

[46] It must be remembered that Niebuhr does not utilize this approach. Indeed, he sharply distinguishes syncretic apologetics, which he contends merges faith and culture, from the miracle apologetics, which isolates faith and culture. Niebuhr would do well to consider that the most rationalistic forms of theology, e.g., Catholic scholasticism and Protestant fundamentalism, are not averse to appealing to the proofs of miracles.

itself to its divine ground and source. Niebuhr quotes Kierkegaard extensively in his endeavor to portray the contingency and ambiguity in the rational enterprise. Indirectly he draws upon the insights of Kant, for many of Kierkegaard's insights are Kantian. It was Kant who propounded that whenever reason tries to penetrate beyond the strictly phenomenal realm, it is involved in hopeless antinomies. Kant at the same time maintained that unless we presuppose a Supreme Being we can give no systematic unity to our experience. Niebuhr is sympathetic with those apologists who argue that the self demands a principle of explanation beyond its capacity to transcend itself if its broken structures of meaning are to be correlated in some intelligible pattern. According to Niebuhr the theologian cannot demonstrate the truth of faith by an appeal either to logic or to the miraculous. One can, however, show that reason is compelled to seek for a criterion that transcends its outermost boundaries in order to attain systematic unity.

> This faith in the sovereignty of a divine creator, judge, and redeemer is not subject to rational proof, because it stands beyond and above the rational coherences of the world and can therefore not be proved by an analysis of these coherences. But a scientific and philosophical analysis of these coherences is not incapable of revealing where they point beyond themselves to a freedom which is not in them, to contradictions between each other which suggest a profounder mystery and meaning beyond them.[47]

---

[47] "Coherence, Incoherence, and Christian Faith" in *Christian Realism and Political Problems*, p. 203.

Chapter III

Niebuhr's Vindication of the Apologetic Principle

General Revelation

The guiding principle of apologetic theology is that there is a possibility of common ground between the Word of God and the self-understanding of the natural person. Apart from this possibility the human person would be unable to apprehend the gospel of Christ. Despite his devastating criticisms of much of the apologetic theology of the past, Reinhold Niebuhr is unequivocal in his judgment that there is a point of connection between the Word of God and human reason, and he finds this connecting point in general revelation. Niebuhr correlates general revelation with common grace just as he correlates special revelation with saving grace. Whereas "revelation" refers more to the noetic content of God's Word, "grace" signifies its redemptive content.

According to Niebuhr all people have in some fashion experienced a reality beyond themselves. All people have had the sense of being confronted with a "wholly other" at the edge of their consciousness. Niebuhr terms this universal experience of God "private revelation" as well as "general revelation." "It is no less universal for being private. Private revelation is the testimony in the consciousness of every person that his life touches a reality beyond himself, a reality deeper and higher than the system of nature in which he stands."[1] Because of private revelation seekers of truth "are able to entertain the more precise revelations of the character and purpose of God as they come to them in the most significant experiences of

---

[1] *Human Nature*, p. 127.

prophetic history."² "Without the public and historical revelation the private experience of God would remain poorly defined and subject to caprice. Without the private revelation of God, the public and historical revelation would not gain credence."³

Niebuhr maintains that the general revelation of God contains three elements. First there is the sense of a "reverence for a majesty and of dependence upon an ultimate source of being."⁴ Second, there is a "sense of moral obligation laid upon one from beyond oneself and of moral unworthiness before a judge."⁵ The third element is the longing for forgiveness. These three elements reflect an encounter with God as Creator, Judge, and Redeemer respectively. These elements comprise the basic noetic content of general revelation. Apart from special revelation this content is blurred and distorted by the human being's idolatrous pretension.

Niebuhr gives special emphasis to the sense of moral obligation, which he variously terms "conscience," the "law of love" and the "*justitia originalis.*" He concedes that the content of conscience is very much conditioned by time and place. "Yet the minimal terms of our obligations to our neighbors, incorporated, for instance, in the prohibition of murder, theft and adultery, are fairly universal."⁶ Niebuhr supports Hume's observation "that the 'preference for benevolence over self-regard' was universal, certainly more universal than actual benevolence."⁷

The basic content of conscience is a sense of obligation to love our neighbor coupled with a sense of not fulfilling this obligation. It is because we are aware of our moral inadequacy that it is possible for us to be convicted of sin. It is because we have a sense of our unworthiness that we are able to respond to the divine offer of forgiveness. According to Niebuhr the "uneasy conscience" is the

---

² *Ibid.*

³ *Ibid.*

⁴ *Ibid.*, p. 131.

⁵ *Ibid.*

⁶ *The Self and the Dramas of History* (New York: Charles Scribner's Sons, 1955), p. 14.

⁷ *Ibid.*

"point of contact" between the person in sin and the gospel: "It is because there is an uneasiness in every human heart about the relativity of every human good (a covert revelation of something beyond itself) that the divine word can be heard and related to human experience."[8] Indeed, "Faith in Christ could find no lodging place in the human soul, were it not uneasy about the contrast between its true and its present state; though this same faith in Christ also clarifies that contrast."[9]

Niebuhr finds in general revelation a basic continuity between the Word of God and human reason, hopes, and aspirations. In Niebuhr's view the Logos that is present in the creation is the same Logos that became incarnate in Christ. Although we are not capable of committing ourselves to Christ through our own power, we are able to hear and understand this Word by virtue of the fact that human reason participates in the Logos of creation. We aspire toward the gospel because our spirit is in constant touch with the divine spirit. To be sure, the human quest will always result in the adoration of something that is less than the unconditional if we fail to encounter God in the concreteness of His historical revelation. Yet despite a certain tension and even friction between human hopes and aspirations and the gospel, there is still an underlying continuity which makes the apologetic task feasible. If we were incapable of seeking as well as apprehending that which is greater than ourselves, the apologist would not be able to guide the unbeliever to Christ. It is because God has revealed Himself in the creation that it is possible for humans to appropriate His special revelation in history. It is because God has encountered all people in their private experience that there is a possibility of common ground between the gospel of God and the meaning orientations of a seeking humanity.

Although Niebuhr finds a point of contact between the gospel and the natural person in general revelation, at one place he ap-

---

[8] Reinhold Niebuhr, "The Contribution of Paul Tillich," *Religion in Life*, 6, no. 4 (Autumn, 1937), p. 576.

[9] *Human Nature*, p. 266; cf. *Human Destiny*, p. 117.

pears to limit this contact to only a certain group of people. In one of his books he draws a distinction between the "children of light" and the "children of darkness" and maintains that only the former have a sense of moral obligation to a higher power. "The children of darkness are evil because they know no law beyond the self. They are wise, though evil, because they understand the power of self-interest."[10] The children of light are different since "they have some conception of a higher law than their own will."[11] Since apart from an uneasy conscience there can be no meeting ground between faith and unbelief, Niebuhr cuts the ground from under an apologetics aimed at converting Nazis, nihilists, and the other groups whom he denominates "children of darkness." Perhaps Niebuhr would say that at one time in their lives the children of darkness had a moral sense but because of the degree of their idolatrous presumption this sense has been darkened beyond recognition. Whatever Niebuhr's interpretation might be, it is safe to conclude that he does not regard an apologetics directed to the children of darkness as feasible. Niebuhr hints at this very strongly when he says in a slightly different context: "The wise men who see the logic of history so plainly always live under the illusion that the men of power can finally be persuaded to see what they see."[12]

It is interesting to note that both Tillich and Richardson state what Niebuhr only implies, viz., that there can be no apologia intended for nihilists and cynics. At one place Tillich asserts that we have a common court of judgment with secular humanists but not with nihilists whom he labels the "new pagans." "In the face of Paganism there is no such thing as apologetics, but only the struggle for existence or non-existence, which prophetic Monotheism has always carried on against demonic Polytheism."[13] In his *Christian*

---

[10] Reinhold Niebuhr, *The Children of Light and the Children of Darkness* (New York: Charles Scribner's Sons, 1944), p.10.

[11] *Ibid.*, pp. 10, 11.

[12] Reinhold Niebuhr, *Reflections On the End of An Era* (New York: Charles Scribner's Sons, 1934), p. 34.

[13] Paul Tillich, *The Interpretation of History*, trans. N.A.Rasetzki and Elsa L. Talmey (New York: Charles Scribner's Sons, 1936), p. 43.

Apologetics Alan Richardson distinguishes four types of moderns: the humanists, Marxists, indifferent secularists, and nihilists. He claims that an apologetical approach will be useful in dealing with the humanists and Marxists but not with the other types.[14]

> The humanists' high regard for truth and value and the Marxists' eagerness for social justice alike prove to be highly significant "points of connection," and there is thus in each case a mutually acknowledged criterion, however small may be the area of agreement when the discussion begins.[15]

But regarding the cynics and nihilists he says: "Only the uncompromising confrontation with the disturbing Gospel proclamation is likely to have any effect upon them."[16]

Dialectical Theology

Niebuhr's theology is oriented about the fact that the self is in dialogue with itself, with other selves, and with God. The capacity of the self to engage in such a dialogue is a striking testimony of its freedom over nature, including its own nature. Niebuhr terms this rational capacity of the self to transcend both itself and nature "spirit." "Spirit" is the creative aspect of the self; it is a sign that the human person is made in God's image. According to Niebuhr the human spirit is in constant dialogue with the divine Spirit. It is through this dialogue that mortals attain valid knowledge both about God and themselves. Niebuhr's theology might be rightly termed "dialectical."[17]

---

[14] It is interesting to observe that Niebuhr also regards the Marxists as persons with whom we have something in common. However, he draws a distinction between the authentic Marxist and the Stalinist, the latter whom he categorizes as a child of darkness. In a more recent statement on Communism he says regarding its conflict with the West: "We are dealing with a conflict between contending forces which have no common presuppositions." Reinhold Niebuhr, *The Irony of American History* (New York: Charles Scribner's Sons, 1952), p. 173.

[15] Alan Richardson, *Christian Apologetics* (New York: Harper & Brothers, 1947), p. 27.

[16] *Ibid.*, p. 26.

[17] For a technical definition of dialectical thinking see Paul L. Lehmann, "The Direction of Theology Today," *Union Seminary Quarterly Review*, 3, no. 1 (Nov., 1947), p. 6.

It is possible to detect Martin Buber's influence on Niebuhr's interpretation of the dialogue between divinity and humanity. Buber envisages this dialogue as an encounter between the "I" (the self) and the "Thou" (God). According to Buber, this encounter is analogous to that between the self and another person. Niebuhr reveals his affinity with Buber by contending that just as we cannot make contact with another person unless he or she speaks to us, so our contact with God is contingent upon His Word.[18] Yet Niebuhr diverges from Buber by maintaining that although God speaks to humans through conscience and history, only in Christ does He speak decisively. Niebuhr also holds that only in Christ is a person sufficiently enlightened to recognize the full implications of this dialogue. Outside of Christ the dialogue is misconstrued by the human being's darkened reason, and its continuity is intermittently broken by the human being's rebellious will.

The apologetic task is made feasible because of the dialogue (although it is admittedly broken) between the "I" and the "Thou." If there were no such dialogue, the theologian would be unable to make contact with what the unbeliever regards as true. If there were no such encounter, then there would be an invincible barrier between the message of the cross and human self-understanding. The dialectic between time and eternity, the human and the divine, is a necessary presupposition of Niebuhr's apologetic enterprise. It signifies that human beings are able to seek God as well as to respond to God. Unless they are capable of carrying on such a dialogue, unless they are able to respond to the command of God, then any attempt to guide them into a closer relationship with God would be futile.

Niebuhr is poignantly aware that what is commonly designated as "dialectical theology" is quite different from his theology. The "dialectical theology" propounded by Karl Barth denies that the natural person is able to converse with God on any level. For the Barthians the ability of humans to respond to God is derived

---

Lehmann points out that dialectical means "speaking between" and involves both negative and positive affirmations.

[18] For Niebuhr's exposition of this analogy see *Human Nature*, p. 130.

solely from the Word of God; it is not a native endowment. This is to say that if God is known, He is known only through Himself. For Barth the dialectic is between God and the reborn person, or more precisely, between God and His Spirit within the reborn person. Niebuhr gives his support to Tillich's critique of Barthianism entitled "What is Wrong with the 'Dialectic' Theology?"[19] I shall proceed to analyze this essay.

Tillich maintains that the Barthian type of dialectical theology is not really dialectical but rather supernatural. According to Tillich a genuine dialectic theology is centered about a meeting between God and the human person in which "yes" and "no" are mutually involved. But in the so-called "dialectic theology" there is no mutual interaction between God and human beings, but only a contradiction. "That is why this theology is not dialectic."[20] Authentic dialectic thinking concurs with the supernatural kind of thinking that a purely divine possibility cannot be interpreted as a human possibility. But dialectic thinking insists that the question about the divine possibility is a human possibility. It further maintains "that no question could be asked about the divine possibility unless a divine answer, even if preliminary and scarcely intelligible, were not always already available."[21] Indeed, in order to be able to ask about God one "must already have experienced God as the goal of a possible question."[22] Tillich and Niebuhr agree that the perennial encounter between divinity and humanity accounts for the fact that people seek and ask about God. It must be said that Tillich's conception of this encounter is more impersonal and mystical than Niebuhr's.[23] Tillich views the dialectical process in the following manner:

---

[19] See Reinhold Niebuhr, "The Contribution of Paul Tillich," *Religion in Life*, 6, no. 4 (Autumn, 1937), pp 575-577.

[20] Paul Tillich, "What is Wrong with The 'Dialectic' Theology?" *The Journal of Religion*, 15, no. 2 (April, 1935), p. 127.

[21] *Ibid.*, p. 137.

[22] *Ibid.*

[23] Tillich seldom uses the term "encounter" and even less the term "dialogue." Within the context of his thought these terms when made to refer to interaction between God and humanity can only be regarded as "metaphorical" rather than "analogical."

> We can find God *in* us only when we rise *above* ourselves. This transcendentalizing act does not signify that we possess the transcendental. The point is that we are in quest of it. But on the other hand this quest is possible only because the transcendental has already dragged us out beyond ourselves as we have received answers which drive us to the quest. The development of this dialectic is the proper aim of philosophy of religion and of the improperly so-called "natural theology."[24]

Niebuhr also sides with Brunner against Barth in their debate regarding the point of contact between God and humanity. Niebuhr is sympathetic with Brunner because this theologian attempts to safeguard the dialectic principle. Yet Niebuhr believes that in this debate Barth is more consistent because Brunner accepts too many of his opponent's presuppositions.[25] I shall proceed to examine this debate in order to understand better the gulf between the apologetic and kerygmatic "dialectical" theologies.

In his essay *Nature and Grace* Brunner maintains that the natural person has a receptivity for the Word of God. Because humans are made in the image of God, they are receptive to words, including the Word of God.[26] While through sin they have lost the capacity to believe the Word, they nevertheless retain a capacity to hear the Word.[27] Niebuhr would go somewhat further in maintaining that humans can also make some effort towards believing the Word.[28] On the whole the positions of Niebuhr and Brunner on this point are strikingly similar. Niebuhr would especially concur in these remarks of Brunner: "The Word of God could not reach a man who had lost his consciousness of God entirely. A man

---

Whereas the connection or likeness between two objects can be rationally determined in the case of an analogy, it can only be intuitively apprehended in a metaphor. Cf. Niebuhr's stricture on Tillich's apologetics, *supra*, pp. 30-31.

[24] Tillich, "What is Wrong with the 'Dialectic' Theology?" *The Journal of Religion*, 15, no. 2 (April 1935), pp. 140-141.

[25] *Human Destiny*, p. 64 n.

[26] Emil Brunner, "Nature and Grace" in *Natural Theology*, trans. Peter Fraenkel, Introduction by John Baillie (London: Geoffrey Bles, Centenary Press, 1946), p. 31.

[27] *Ibid.*, p. 32.

[28] Cf. *Human Destiny*, p. 63.

without conscience cannot be struck by the call 'Repent ye and believe the Gospel.'"[29]

Barth sees in Brunner's position only another variety of synergism. Brunner speaks of a "receptivity for words," but what is the meaning of this "if man can do nothing of himself for his salvation, if it is the Holy Spirit that gives him living knowledge of the word of the Cross?"[30] Barth concludes that Brunner means that lost human beings can do something for their salvation, that therefore this so-called "receptivity for words" is a "capacity for revelation," a capacity to be addressed. Sinful humanity therefore is not saved by grace alone but by grace plus an inner ability to meet or receive the God who is revealed. Barth opposes what Niebuhr and Brunner consider to be the dialectic principle, viz., that it is possible for the natural person to apprehend the Word of God. Apart from this possibility there can be no common ground between the self-understanding of the natural person and the gospel and therefore no valid apologetics in the conventional use of this term.

Niebuhr's dialectical orientation is especially evident in his adherence to the *analogia entis*. This term has more theological significance in Europe than America, possibly because it has not been effectively challenged in this country. It denotes an analogical relation between God and His creation (with special emphasis on the human creation). Niebuhr is continually drawing analogies from the area of human experience in order to describe the workings of God. Niebuhr contends that if we were not able to formulate analogies between God and humanity, there could be no dialectical theology. If our words were not analogous to the Word of God, we could neither hear nor answer the call of God. Barth's position is that the analogous relation between God and His creation does not provide any possibility for knowledge of God, since sin has irremediably marred this relation. Barth does hold, however, that there is an *analogia fidei*, i.e., an analogous relation between God and humanity discernible on the basis of faith.

---

[29] Emil Brunner, "Nature and Grace" in *Natural Theology*, p. 32.

[30] Karl Barth, "No! Answer to Emil Brunner" in *Natural Theology*, p. 79.

Niebuhr's contention that the self is in dialogue with God is only another way of affirming general revelation.[31] The fact that it is possible and indeed inevitable for the natural person to converse with God, albeit in a limited and broken way, is a manifestation of the working of God in creation; it is a sign of common grace. The kerygmatic theologians interpret the dialectical principle differently because they deny the transforming or saving power of general revelation. Niebuhr's position is synergistic, which means that sinful humans can do something for their salvation. The kerygmatic position is more likely to be monergistic: God saves sinners despite and even against their own efforts. The synergistic position presupposes common ground between human self-understanding and the Word of God. The monergistic position is inclined to deny or ignore any common ground, since it regards sinful humanity as helpless apart from the special condescension of God in Jesus Christ.

Existential Disruption

The term "existential disruption" is employed by Tillich rather than Niebuhr, but if used in a certain way it can also denote Niebuhr's view of sin. Sin for Niebuhr means a disruption at the very center of human existence. Yet this disruption is not believed to have destroyed the efficacy of general revelation. It does not wipe out all semblance of common ground between faith and unbelief. It would be well to analyze Niebuhr's conception of sin, since this has much bearing on his apologetical approach.

Even in his earliest writings Niebuhr was painfully aware of the disruptive power of sin in human life, especially in social rela-

---

[31] At one place Niebuhr draws a distinction between the general experience of God and the conversation with God which he links with special revelation. Cf. *Human Nature*, pp. 130-131. On the whole, however, he would tend to subsume the general experience of God within the dialogic scheme, and he would tend to regard only an encounter with God Incarnate as special revelation. His most recent position on the dialectic is expounded in *The Self and the Dramas of History*.

tions.³² Even when his theology was oriented more about value judgments than the message of the cross he was still able to discern the idolatrous pretension that has discolored the creativity of the human race. He held that "human nature is neither lovable nor trustworthy."³³

> The real religious spirit has no illusions about human nature. It knows the heart of man to be sinful. It is therefore not subject to the cynical disillusion into which sentimentality degenerates when it comes into contact with the disappointing facts of human history.³⁴

Niebuhr finds the root of sin is humanity's inveterate unwillingness to acknowledge its finitude and dependence on God. We are tempted to delude ourselves into thinking that we are independent and self-sufficient because of our anxiety over our contingent position. Unlike the animals, we can anticipate the perils of contingency. Moreover, in contradistinction to the animal world, we are free to repudiate our contingency. Because humans are both free and anxious, sin is inevitable. Yet Niebuhr contends that "the anxiety of freedom leads to sin only if the prior sin of unbelief is assumed."³⁵ We could not be tempted unless sin were already present. The false interpretation of life "is not purely the product of the human imagination. It is suggested to man by a force of evil which precedes his own sin."³⁶ Niebuhr finds the locus of this original sin in the myth of the devil. The devil represents "a fallen angel, who fell because he sought to lift himself above his measure and who in turn insinuates temptation into human life."³⁷ Niebuhr elucidates the mysterious complexity of the fact of sin:

---

[32] His classic work on collective sin is *Moral Man and Immoral Society* (New York: Charles Scribner's Sons, 1932). In this work he maintains that collective pride is the most virulent manifestation of sin.

[33] *Does Civilization Need Religion?* (New York: Macmillan, 1927), pp. 41-42.

[34] Reinhold Niebuhr, *The Contribution of Religion to Social Work* (New York: Columbia University Press, 1932), p. 66.

[35] *Human Nature*, p. 252; Cf. pp. 250-1.

[36] *Ibid.* p. 181.

[37] *Ibid.*, p. 254.

> The sin of each individual is preceded by Adam's sin: but even this first sin of history is not the first sin. One may, in other words, go farther back than human history and still not escape the paradoxical conclusion that the situation of finiteness and freedom would not lead to sin if sin were not already introduced into the situation.[38]

Niebuhr concurs with Kierkegaard that sin presupposes itself.[39] The ultimate origin of sin is a mystery.

Niebuhr takes pains to differentiate his view of sin from that of Augustine and the Reformers. He rejects the view that original sin is an inherited corruption. Such a doctrine tends to efface human responsibility for sin. Niebuhr holds that sin is universal but not necessary.

> Sin is to be regarded as neither a necessity of man's nature nor yet as a pure caprice of his will. It proceeds rather from a defect of the will, for which reason it is not completely deliberate; but since it is the will in which the defect is found and the will presupposes freedom the defect cannot be attributed to a taint in man's nature.[40]

Niebuhr also distinguishes his view from that of Tillich, which tends to link sin and finitude too closely. According to Niebuhr the anxiety concerning finitude provides the occasion for sin, but there is no necessary connection. Tillich speaks of sin as an "ontological fate," something that is inherent in the creation. When Tillich refers to Adam's "created goodness" he seems to conceive of a "goodness before creation, before actualization in time."[41] The age of innocence "seems to be a state of potentiality rather than actuality."[42] For Niebuhr the age of innocence has a historical locus (both in the life of individuals and the race).

---

[38] *Ibid.*

[39] *Ibid.*, pp. 251, 252.

[40] *Ibid.*, p. 242.

[41] Reinhold Niebuhr, "Biblical Thought and Ontological Speculation" in *The Theology of Paul Tillich*, ed. Charles W. Kegley and Robert W. Bretall (New York: Macmillan, 1952), p. 223.

[42] *Ibid.*

> It is important to recognize the historical fact...that in both the individual and collective life of mankind there is a historical period in which there is a considerable harmony of life with life or harmony of life within itself. Increasing freedom disturbs this harmony. But it also creates the possibility of wider harmonies and larger communities.[43]

I will not take more space to expound Niebuhr's conception of the source of sin, since what is most important to this thesis is the degree of corruption that sin causes. Niebuhr believes that every part of every person is tainted by sin, but he interprets this taint as a discoloring rather than an obfuscation. Sin circumscribes human freedom, but it does not destroy this freedom. Sin distorts our reasoning process, but it does not subvert this process. The natural person is still free to respond to God and also to apprehend God.

> Neither the finiteness of the human mind nor the sinful corruption of the mind or the "ideological taint" in all human culture can completely efface the human capacity for the apprehension of the true wisdom. Since there can be no total corruption of truth or virtue there is always a residual desire for the true wisdom, and the real God and the final revelation of the meaning of life, below and above the sinful tendency to build a world of meaning around ourselves as the center.[44]

Niebuhr believes that the human person's original desire for truth has not been destroyed by sin. Yet with Augustine he is staunch in his conviction that unless the grace of God channels and thereby fulfills this desire, this desire cannot save us from our predicament. Apart from the transforming power of God our native predilection for truth can result only in a perverse type of idolatry. People desire the truth and are free to decide for the truth, but unless the truth confronts them in the person of Jesus Christ, they inevitably become shackled to delusion.

Even after one becomes a Christian, Niebuhr insists, existential disruption remains. "Sin is overcome in principle but not in

---

[43] *Ibid.*, pp. 223-4.
[44] *Human Destiny*, p. 63.

fact."[45] By this he means that Christians are able to free themselves from the damning consequences of sin by accepting divine forgiveness. Yet the presence of sin still lingers on even in our most commendable actions. Christians are justified because Christ took upon Himself the penalty of sin by dying on a cross. Yet Christians remain sinners, for the possibility of perfect love, which was incarnate in Christ, is realized within us only in discontinuous moments of prayer and decision. Niebuhr holds that the presence of sin in the life of the Christian will be eradicated only at the end of history when Christ comes again in order to usher in the kingdom of God.

Niebuhr faults Roman Catholic theology for not taking seriously the extent of the disruption of human nature. Catholic theologians speak of an original righteousness that was lost in the fall, but they hold that a natural justice remains, which is for the most part uncorrupted by sin. The supernatural virtues have been destroyed, but there still exist natural virtues, which are essentially free of the taint of sin. Niebuhr holds that there is "no uncorrupted natural law, just as there is no completely lost original justice."[46] "The freedom of man sets every standard of justice under higher possibilities, and the sin of man perennially insinuates contingent and relative elements into the supposedly absolute standards of human reason."[47] Niebuhr also roundly criticizes the Roman Catholic contention that grace overcomes sin in fact as well as in principle. Such a contention, he claims, can result only in a type of pharisaism and even in a type of sentimental optimism.

Niebuhr is especially distrustful of Protestant liberal theology, which tends to ignore or explain away the disruption in humanity's being. According to him the liberals "sought the cause of historical evil in ignorance, in social institutions, in everything" but in the human person.[48] It was because liberal theologians did not discern the radical evil within humanity that they were betrayed into a false

---

[45] *Ibid.*, p. 49.

[46] *Human Nature*, p. 281.

[47] *Ibid.*

[48] Reinhold Niebuhr, "The False Defense of Christianity," *Christianity and Crisis*, 10, no. 10 (June 12, 1950), p. 73.

apologetics.⁴⁹ Indeed, if we fail to perceive that behind the doubts of our hearers lies an inherent antagonism towards the gospel, we will tend to compromise the faith by trying to make it consistent with their viewpoint rather than attempting to overthrow their viewpoint.

If Niebuhr sternly rejects the rationalist approach to the problem of sin (whether this be in a Catholic or a liberal guise), he just as adamantly repudiates the Reformation and neo-Reformation views. These types of theologies tend to exaggerate human sinfulness. By stressing the corruption of human reason, they tend to undercut the point of contact between the human nous and the divine logos. By emphasizing the bondage of the will, they deny that a person even has the freedom to respond to the Word of God. They break the paradoxical unity of God's elective action and a person's free decision by conceiving of humanity as being determined either by sin or by God. "In radical Protestantism the very image of God in man is believed to be destroyed. And when Protestant thought recoils from such extravagance, it looks for the remnant of man's original goodness in insignificant aspects of human behaviour."⁵⁰ Niebuhr cites as an example of this attempt to locate the "imago Dei" in insignificant aspects of behavior Karl Barth's concession "that man is man and not a cat."⁵¹

While insistent that the revelation in creation has been seriously disrupted by human sin, Niebuhr does not wish to imply its destruction. The general revelation persists despite its broken and distorted character. There is still a dialogue with God despite the fact that sin blurs and at times even deadens the voice of God. Niebuhr holds that if there were no continuity between God and humanity within the discontinuity wrought by sin, then there could be no point of connection between faith and unbelief. Then there could be no semblance of common ground between the gospel of Christ and human self-understanding. Niebuhr faults the classical

---

⁴⁹ *Faith and History* (New York: Charles Scribner's Sons, 1949), p. 146.
⁵⁰ *Human Nature*, p. 269.
⁵¹ *Ibid.*, n.

apologists for not taking seriously the disruption brought about by sin. Yet he equally opposes those whom he labels "obscurantists" for not taking seriously the work of common grace within the life of sinful humanity. Niebuhr upbraids those theologians who take sin lightly because they are in danger of compromising the faith whenever they attempt to defend it before the world. He distances himself from those theologians who hold to a doctrine of total depravity because they tend to subvert the apologetic enterprise. Niebuhr believes that one cannot have a valid apologetics unless one has a correct understanding of human nature. He also believes that such an understanding of human nature makes the apologetic enterprise possible and even necessary.

Chapter IV

Apologetics as a Means of Validating the Faith

Niebuhr sees apologetics as a means of validating the truth of faith. Our hearers can come to know this truth only by commitment, but we can establish its relevance by demonstrating how it is validated in experience. If we could not validate this truth, then it would have no relevance to our situation. It would be on the same level as a mystical truth, i.e., it would defy intelligibility.

> Since such faith is by commitment, the interpretation of the faith can not follow as a rational deduction from the given facts. Yet faith can not be irrational or capricious. It must validate itself as an interpretation of the facts of existence.[1]

It is not always easy to discern what Niebuhr means by "validation." At one place he says that the gospel is not "proved to be true by rational analysis."[2] But then again he declares that it "can be empirically verified as the truth."[3] What he seems to mean is that although the truth of faith can be shown to be supported by the facts of experience, this support is of such a nature that it cannot compel one to assent, as in the case of strictly logical proofs. According to Niebuhr we can verify the faith, but we cannot seal this faith in the hearts of our hearers. We can demonstrate the relevance of the faith, but we cannot establish its reality.

---

[1] *The Self and the Dramas of History* (New York: Charles Scribner's Sons, 1955), p. 91. It is important to note that Niebuhr's attempt to validate the faith springs from his belief that the Bible makes a similar attempt. Cf. "Coherence, Incoherence, and Christian Faith" in *Christian Realism and Political Problems* (New York: Charles Scribner's Sons, 1953), pp 185, 186.

[2] *Faith and History* (New York: Charles Scribner's Sons, 1949) p. 151.

[3] *The Self and the Dramas of History*, p. 92.

Niebuhr holds that there are two types of validation, the negative and the positive. The negative validation of the faith consists in showing how reason becomes involved in hopeless antinomies unless it is grounded in the Word of God. The positive validation consists in correlating the broken insights of culture and the revelatory insights of faith. It is significant to note that Niebuhr makes the positive approach contingent upon the negative approach: "There is no way of validating the truth of the gospel until men have discovered the error which appears in their final truth."[4] We can therefore safely state that Niebuhr's overall position is eristical. This is to say that his dominant intention is to undercut the self-understanding of secular humanity, but he does this in such a way as to show how one can know oneself truly only in the light of revelation.

Negative Validation

For Niebuhr our task as apologists is to uncover the contradictions within the various alternatives to Christianity. Such an approach does not prove the gospel, but it does demonstrate its relevance. We cannot arrive at the Christian position through rational analysis; yet only on the basis of this position can we give rational unity to our experience. Only the Christian position enables us to make sense out of our existence whereas other positions breed confusion.

> Whether in the period when the Gospel of Christ was first proclaimed and accepted, or in our own day, the acceptance of such a gospel is always experienced as a miracle of revelation in the sense that the relation between God and man which it establishes is not the achievement of a rational analysis of life. Yet it is felt to be a new wisdom and power. From its standpoint it is possible to "make sense" out of life;

---

[4] *Human Destiny*, p. 210.

whereas alternative approaches either destroy the sense of life entirely or make false sense of it.[5]

One of the alternatives that Niebuhr tries to counter is the optimistic faith in history, which has pervaded nearly all levels of our culture. This optimism "makes the central message of the gospel, dealing with sin, grace, forgiveness and justification, seem totally irrelevant."[6] The naturalistic metaphysics that is correlated with this optimistic faith "reduces the time and eternity problem to meaninglessness."[7] The task of the theologian is to overthrow this modern faith so that its adherents might come to appreciate the relevance and meaningfulness of the Christian faith. Niebuhr seeks to uproot the optimism in our culture by appealing to the "tragic" and "brutal" facts of history. He cogently shows how the only peace that has ever been realized in history has been an "uneasy armistice," a peace made possible only by compromise and coercion. He points to the recent course of human history, which has witnessed the rise of ruthless dictatorships and the threat of total war, in order to underscore his thesis that the faith of modernity rests upon an illusion. Niebuhr attempts to subvert the naturalism in our culture by demonstrating how naturalistic philosophies are unable to explain satisfactorily the capacity of human beings to transcend the natural process. He also questions the confidence of naturalists in the empirical method, which he maintains is not exempt from the ideological taint.

Niebuhr bases a great part of his apologetics on the failure of secular thought to give an adequate account of the self. For Niebuhr the self stands apart from both reason and nature, yet it is circumscribed by reason and nature. Secular thought on the basis of general revelation has perceived some type of relation between the self and its component parts, but it almost invariably obscures this relation. Idealism overemphasizes the power of reason; naturalism overplays the role of the vital impulses; mysticism tends to dissolve

---

[5] *Faith and History*, p. 141.
[6] *Human Nature*, p. 145.
[7] *Ibid.*

the relationship of the self to its parts. Only when human reason is enlightened by special revelation can it appreciate the subtleties and intricacies of human selfhood. Carnell gives an astute paraphrase of Niebuhr's position on this point:

> Natural revelation sets the problem for man, and special revelation solves it. Man senses by nature that he stands too completely outside of both nature and himself to be understood in terms of either reason or nature. But without special revelation to enlighten him as to the exact demands of eternity, either reason is underscored too strongly or too lightly; or nature is made either all or nothing; or reason and nature remain in an unbalanced, unexplained ratio. Special revelation breaks through historical limitations to tell us the mind of God on the meaning of both man and history.[8]

Although Niebuhr's apologetics contains many original elements, it is interesting to note its similarity to that of Kierkegaard. In his *The Point of View* Kierkegaard asserts that there can be no direct communication of the Christian message because an illusion stands in the way. This illusion is that most people already believe themselves to be Christians. The task of the theologian is to understand the other person's self-understanding which engenders such illusions and then try to overthrow it.[9] Niebuhr believes that the theologian must strive to undercut the illusions that sustain the secularists in their search for security and thereby clear the way for faith. These illusions as Niebuhr sees them are the irresistibility of progress and human perfectibility.

Another theologian who adheres to the eristical method (but not exclusively) and who has exerted an influence on Niebuhr is Tillich. Tillich's eristics is not so evident in his *Systematic Theology*, but it is conspicuous in many of his essays. In "The Protestant Message and the Man of Today" he holds that the first form that the

---

[8] Edward John Carnell, *The Theology of Reinhold Niebuhr* (Grand Rapids, Mich.: Eerdmans, 1951), p. 61.

[9] Søren Kierkegaard, *The Point of View*, trans. Walter Lowrie (London: Oxford University Press, 1939), pp. 27-41.

message of the Protestant Church should take is the destruction of "the secret reservations harbored by the modern man which prevent him from accepting resolutely the limits of his human existence."[10] Tillich admonishes the church not to proclaim its truths directly, since modern people have doubts about these truths. Instead, the church should try to remove these doubts and reservations. In another essay Tillich recommends that the church try to destroy or uproot false stumbling blocks so that the secularist can accept the true stumbling block.[11] In contradistinction to nineteenth-century apologists Tillich does not try to remove doubts and stumbling blocks by proving the credibility of the faith, although he does try to show that the Christian message does not contravene scientific knowledge. For the most part, his intention is to undercut the false foundations that nurture these doubts and thereby bring his hearers to the "boundary situation" or the "abyss of reason." It is then when they experience the threat of non-being that they will be ready to hear and decide for the message of the "New Being."[12] It is difficult to distinguish Niebuhr's and Tillich's approaches on this level except in the realm of terminology.

Niebuhr's negative validation of the faith is also remarkably similar to Brunner's approach. Brunner believes that what is needed is a reevaluation of the underlying purpose of apologetics. Apologetics in the past has always been envisaged in terms of a defense of Christianity at the bar of reason. Brunner says, "Actually...what matters is not 'defense' but 'attack' – the *attack*, namely, of the Church on the opposing positions of unbelief, superstition, or misleading ideologies."[13] Rather than proving the truth of faith, we should spend our energies in unmasking the untruth of paganism. In his attempt to transmute apologetics from a defensive to an of-

---

[10] Paul Tillich, *The Protestant Era*, trans. James Luther Adams (Chicago: University of Chicago Press, 1948), p. 203.

[11] Tillich, "Communicating the Gospel," *Union Seminary Quarterly Review*, 7, no. 4 (June, 1952), p. 11.

[12] See Tillich's essay in "Religion and the Intellectuals," *Partisan Review*, 17, no. 3 (March, 1950), pp. 254-56.

[13] Emil Brunner, *The Christian Doctrine of God*, trans. Olive Wyon (Philadelphia: Westminster Press, 1950), p. 98.

fensive enterprise Brunner quotes St. Paul: "We destroy arguments and every proud obstacle to the knowledge of God, and take every thought captive to obey Christ" (2 Cor. 10:5).[14] He might also have quoted Niebuhr: "The Christian Church must bear witness against every form of pride and vainglory, whether in the secular or in the Christian culture."[15] With Niebuhr and Tillich, Brunner believes that only when unbelievers have been driven from the false security of their unbelief will they be ready to embrace the authentic security proffered by the gospel.

Niebuhr's endeavor to validate the Christian faith by undercutting secular alternatives to the faith also has some affinity with Alan Richardson's approach. Richardson sharply questions the pretended objectivity of secular philosophers, especially those that claim to adhere to the scientific method. According to him every worldview is based upon some faith-principle or value judgment. This faith-principle determines the categories by which one selects and interprets the data of experience. No philosopher can claim to possess objectively verifiable truth because this claim is contingent upon a subjective bias. Richardson quotes from Marx and the historicists in order to underscore the determining power of faith-principles. According to Richardson a faith-principle must be judged by its ability to give rational unity to the whole of experience.[16] The biblical faith-principle most nearly approximates the synoptic or overarching perspective that reason demands.

Niebuhr uses this type of approach in his critique of scientific empiricism – the dominant method of a naturalistic metaphysics. He avers that although science can give detailed accounts of the causal relation of isolated events, it cannot give us a synoptic picture "without introducing presuppositions which are not immediately apparent in the facts and can be found in them only after they have been suggested by the predisposition of the observer."[17] The

---

[14] *Ibid.*, p. 101.

[15] Reinhold Niebuhr, "The Christian Witness in the Social and National Order" in *Christian Realism and Political Problems*, p. 111.

[16] Alan Richardson, *Christian Apologetics* (New York: Harper & Brothers, 1947), p. 231.

[17] *Reflections on the End of an Era* (New York: Charles Scribner's Sons, 1934), p. 194.

ideological taint is discernible "in even the most scientific observations of social scientists."[18] Niebuhr says regarding the procedure in the social sciences: "Every larger frame of meaning, which serves the observer of historical events in correlating the events into some kind of pattern, is a structure of faith rather than of science, in the sense that the scientific procedures must presuppose the framework and it can therefore not be merely their consequence."[19] He suggests that the faith-principles of the naturalistic empiricists are inadequate, since they do not take into consideration the necessity of the role of faith in the empirical method. These empiricists fail "to recognize that every search for truth begins with a presupposition of faith."[20] They can see the contingency in other positions, but very seldom do they acknowledge the contingency in their own positions. They are even less prone to acknowledge that this contingency is in part rooted in wilful self-interest. The biblical faith-principle takes into consideration the relativity and self-interest in all positions, including the Christian position, and therefore most nearly satisfies what people know to be true in their experience.

Positive Validation

Although Niebuhr bases most of his case on the negative validation of the faith, he nevertheless believes that there is a positive apologetic task as well. Just as the negative approach consists in uncovering the antinomies and contradictions in secular positions, so the positive approach consists in correlating the broken insights of culture and the revelatory insights of faith. "Such a correlation validates the truth of faith insofar as it proves it to be a source and center of an interpretation of life, more adequate than alternative interpretations, because it comprehends all of life's antinomies and contradictions into a system of meaning and is conducive to a re-

---

[18] "Ideology and the Scientific Method" in *Christian Realism and Political Problems*, p. 75.

[19] *Faith and History*, p. 119.

[20] Reinhold Niebuhr, *Christianity and Power Politics* (New York: Charles Scribner's Sons, 1940), p. 221.

newal of life."[21] It can be seen that the positive validation is directly related to the negative validation. Whereas the latter predicates the overthrow of alternative positions, the positive approach consists in upholding the Christian position. Because these approaches are only two aspects of the same general approach, Niebuhr's sharp distinction between them is perhaps a cause for confusion.

Niebuhr points out that in pursuing the task of correlating the truth of faith with other truth the theologian is subject to three errors. Each error tends to undermine the redemptive power of faith. "The first error is to regard the truth of faith as capable of simple correlation with any system of rational coherence and as validated by such a correlation."[22] Such an approach would necessarily syncretize the faith with secular thought, and synthesis predicates compromise. Niebuhr accuses liberal Protestantism of correlating faith and culture in this syncretic manner. "The second error arises when the effort is made to guard the uniqueness of the truth of faith and to prevent its absorption into a general system of knowledge by insisting that Christian truth is miraculously validated and has no relation to any truth otherwise known."[23] In Niebuhr's judgment Protestant literalism is particularly prone to this error: "Failure to relate the truth of faith to other knowledge and experience furthermore leads to a cultural obscurantism which denies the obvious truths about life and history, discovered by modern scientific disciplines."[24] "The third error…is to validate the truth of faith but to explicate it rationally in such a way that mystery is too simply resolved into ostensible rational intelligibility."[25] This error characterizes Roman Catholic scholasticism. Niebuhr concludes:

> If the truth of faith merely becomes a "fact" of history, attested by a miracle, or validated by ecclesiastical authority, it

---

[21] *Faith and History*, p. 165.

[22] *Ibid.*

[23] *Ibid.*, p. 166.

[24] *Ibid.*, p. 167.

[25] *Ibid.*

no longer touches the soul profoundly. If it is made into a truth of reason which is validated by its coherence with a total system of rational coherence, it also loses its redemptive power. The truth of the Christian Gospel is apprehended at the very limit of all systems of meaning. It is only from that position that it has the power to challenge the complacency of those who have completed life too simply, and the despair of those who can find no meaning in life.[26]

It is interesting to compare Niebuhr's attempt at correlation with that of Tillich. Tillich's method of correlation is based upon the presupposition that all people are seeking the "New Being" which can heal their disruption. According to Tillich, humans are aware of what they need, but they do not possess the reality that can satisfy their needs. They are able to raise the right questions, but they are still seeking the answers to these questions. The method of correlation "tries to correlate the questions implied in the situation with the answers implied in the message."[27] By the "situation" Tillich means "man's creative self-interpretation in a special period."[28] The questions that are raised implicitly or explicitly in the philosophy, art, and literature of any given period find their solution in the event of Christ. Tillich acknowledges that many people have not yet been stirred into asking the questions to which the kerygma gives the answer. It is up to the minister therefore to guide them toward the more universal questions so that they will more readily apprehend the Christian answer. This is the approach that is called for in work among primitive peoples. "We seek to answer *their* questions and in doing so we, at the same time, slowly transform their existence so that they come to ask the questions to which the Christian message gives the answer."[29]

Niebuhr diverges from the Tillichian scheme in contending that the Christian message answers only those questions that are

---

[26] *Ibid.*, p. 170.

[27] Tillich, *Systematic Theology* (Chicago: University of Chicago Press, 1951), 1:8.

[28] *Ibid.*, p. 4.

[29] Tillich, "Communicating the Gospel," *Union Seminary Quarterly Review*, 7, no. 4 (June, 1952), p. 6.

"Christological." By a Christological question Niebuhr means a question that regards history as "potentially meaningful but as still awaiting the full disclosure and fulfillment of its meaning."[30] Niebuhr holds that Christological questions have arisen only in the Western world, since this world is for the most part messianic, i.e., it awaits the full disclosure of meaning. Eastern cultures do not expect a Christ, for in these cultures "the meaning of life is explained from the standpoint of either nature or supernature in such a way that a transcendent revelation of history's meaning is not regarded as either possible or necessary."[31]

> Nothing is so incredible as an answer to an unasked question. One half of the world has regarded the Christian answer to the problem of life and history as "foolishness" because it had no questions for which the Christian revelation was the answer and no longings and hopes which that revelation fulfilled. The cultures of this half of the world were non-Messianic because they were non-historical.[32]

More recently Niebuhr has further qualified his method of correlation by maintaining that the questions of modern culture cannot be satisfactorily conjoined with the Christian message. The reason for this is that these questions do not take into consideration human misery and guilt.

> The modern "Socratic" culture has not stated the questions for which such a faith is the answer, even if it acknowledged the reality and the "dignity" of human selfhood. It did not do so because it prided itself on the "dignity" of man but never came to terms with the "misery" of man.[33]

It would seem that Niebuhr in contradistinction to Tillich believes that most people today are unable to formulate questions that are relevant to the Christian answer. Niebuhr links the method of correlation more explicitly to the eristical method than does Til-

---

[30] *Human Destiny*, p. 4.

[31] *Ibid.*, pp. 4, 5.

[32] *Ibid.*, p. 6.

[33] Reinhold Niebuhr, "Christ vs. Socrates," *The Saturday Review*, 37 (Dec. 18, 1954), p. 8.

lich. Niebuhr would first try to undercut and overthrow the questions of his hearers in order to make them aware of the ideological character of their reasoning. Only then when they perceive the illusion that has nurtured their questions are they enabled to ask the questions for which Christ is the answer. It must be pointed out that even then the Christian answer negates as well as fulfills these questions in that they contain an element of sinful pretension.[34] It would seem that Tillich envisages a correlation that is more direct and natural.

Both Niebuhr and Tillich emphasize the mystery and incommensurability of the Christian answer, but Niebuhr seems to stress this more. According to Niebuhr the reason why there cannot be any simple correlation between the truths of reason and faith is that these truths are on different levels. The truths of faith "transcend the categories of human reason."[35] The gospel or the kerygma is something more than a structure of meaning; it is the criterion or ground of all meaning. Because of this transcendent quality, it cannot be fully appropriated until reason has been completely transformed by grace. This transformation is not a possibility within history. The Christian answer in contradistinction to the answers of secular thought has an eschatological orientation.[36]

Besides the method of correlation Niebuhr speaks of another kind of positive validation of the faith. This is the pragmatic proof, which appears to be a reflection of Niebuhr's liberal heritage. At a very early time Niebuhr maintained: "Religion, in the final analysis, is justified by life, by morally potent and poetically vital life."[37] And again: "Redemption may involve more than moral fruits...but the moral test must be applied. Without it redemption sinks into magic, which, because it has no objective and historical tests to support its validity, authenticates itself by claiming magical revela

---

[34] *Human Destiny*, p. 215.

[35] *Ibid.*, p. 149.

[36] *Faith and History*, p. 214.

[37] Reinhold Niebuhr, "Christian Faith in the Modern World" in *Ventures In Belief*, ed. Henry P. Van Dusen (New York: Charles Scribner's Sons, 1930), p. 22.

tion in its support."[38] Although Niebuhr has since given much emphasis to historical proofs, he has never abandoned the pragmatic proof. He admonishes the apologist not to point to superior Christian virtues, but one can point to the obvious change in vision and purpose that faith brings about. Niebuhr holds that Christianity must be finally "validated by a witness of lives which have been obviously remade by the power of God's judgment and forgiveness."[39] Niebuhr nowhere associates the pragmatic argument with the negative validation, but it would probably be a correct appraisal of his position that not until one has discerned the limits of human reason and the corruption of the human will can one appreciate the moral fruits of the Christian religion.

Relation of Apologetics to Commitment

Niebuhr takes pains to point out that although apologists can infer from experience the validity of the truth of faith, they cannot implant this truth in the minds of their hearers. Niebuhr contends that "this faith may be justified but can not be established by inference."[40] No analysis of the contradictions in alternative positions can persuade one "to believe that Christ is the key to the ultimate mystery and to the meaning of his own life."[41] What apologetics does do is to establish the relevance of the faith, thereby enabling the seeker after truth to make a meaningful commitment. Apologetics can prepare the way for a decision, but it cannot guarantee this decision. Apologists can lead one up to the faith, but they cannot "rationally force" one to accept this faith.[42]

---

[38] Reinhold Niebuhr, "Christianity and Redemption" in *Whither Christianity*, ed. Lynn Harold Hough (New York: Harper & Brothers, 1929), p. 114.

[39] Reinhold Niebuhr, "The Christian Witness in a Secular Age," *The Christian Century*, 70, no. 29 (July 22, 1953), p. 843. Cf. *An Interpretation of Christian Ethics*, (New York: Harper & Brothers, 1935), pp. 214-15.

[40] *The Self and the Dramas of History*, p. 226.

[41] *Ibid.*

[42] *Faith and History*, p. 101.

In Niebuhr's view an intelligible apologetics prepares the way for commitment by bringing one to the edge of despair, what Tillich would call the "abyss of reason." Even at a very early period Niebuhr was convinced that one must first experience the anxiety of despair before one can be prompted to embrace the security proffered by Christ: "Religion is the hope that grows out of despair. It is the ultimate optimism which follows in the wake of a thorough pessimism."[43] He places his finger on the source of the modern ailment: "One reason why our generation is not religious is that it has been too sentimental to be thoroughly pessimistic. It has never looked into the bottomless abyss, on the edge of which all the citadels of faith are built."[44] In a more recent work he avers: "The truth contained in the gospel is not found in human wisdom. Yet it may be found at the point where human wisdom and human goodness acknowledge their limits; and creative despair induces faith."[45] Yet Niebuhr is aware that there is more than one type of despair. He contrasts the "creative despair" that induces faith with the "sorrow of the world," which finds no answer to the torment that rocks the human spirit.[46] Niebuhr acknowledges that apologists by undercutting the beliefs of their hearers may "inflict a mortal wound."[47] This is to say they may drive their hearers into a permanent nihilism and cynicism, which is even further from faith than moral or spiritual complacency. Yet he insists that "it is nevertheless important from the standpoint of faith to puncture the idolatrous pretensions of cultures."[48] Although the critique of cultural pretensions may drive some into perpetual despair, it "may prompt others to embrace Christ as the key to the mystery."[49]

---

[43] *The Contribution of Religion to Social Work* (New York: Columbia University Press, 1932), p. 73.

[44] *Ibid.*

[45] *Human Destiny*, p. 206.

[46] *Ibid.*, pp. 206, 207. Cf. *Faith and History*, p. 158.

[47] *Faith and History*, p. 154.

[48] *Ibid.*, pp. 154, 155.

[49] *The Self and the Dramas of History*, p. 227.

Niebuhr attributes the fact that some of the despairing believe to the inscrutable grace of God. He reaffirms the Pauline contention "that the recognition of Jesus as the Christ is possible only by the Holy Spirit."[50] The grace of God transmutes the despair of humanity into repentance – the prerequisite of commitment. Niebuhr holds that the commitment of the self is not possible without repentance "because the darkness about the meaning of its existence is due not so much to the finiteness of the self's mind as to pretensions of its heart."[51] This is to say that before we can have faith we must have confessed our idolatrous presumption and our need of forgiveness. Niebuhr cogently analyzes the subtle relation between faith, repentance, and grace:

> Such faith must be grounded in repentance; for it presupposes a contrite recognition of the elements of pretension and false completion in all forms of human virtue, knowledge and achievement. It is a gift of grace because neither the faith nor the repentance required for the knowledge of the true God, revealed in the Cross and the resurrection, can be attained by taking thought. The self must lose itself to find itself in faith and repentance; but it does not find itself unless it be apprehended from beyond itself.[52]

Since Niebuhr believes that the Holy Spirit acts upon the despair and uncertainty brought about by an apology, we can infer that Niebuhr conceives of an apology as in some sense a "means of grace." This signifies a marked divergence from the classical Protestant view that only the Word and the sacraments are the appointed means by which the Holy Spirit works. Niebuhr rejects the traditional view as representing "an intolerable confinement of the freedom of God within human limits."[53] It is difficult to ascertain whether Niebuhr envisages apologetic conversation as a means of common or special grace. At times it would appear that he conceives of apologetics as a means of common grace, which prepares

---

[50] *Faith and History*, p. 146.
[51] *The Self and the Dramas of History*, p. 242.
[52] *Faith and History*, p. 151.
[53] *Human Destiny*, p. 208.

APOLOGETICS AS A MEANS OF VALIDATING THE FAITH 65

one for the sermon. Common grace working through the apology leads one to the edge of despair and special grace working through the message of Christ converts despair into repentance. It is doubtful, however, whether Niebuhr would draw such a sharp distinction between an apology and the message of Christ, since he attempts to state the message within the apology. Again, it must be said that Niebuhr believes that it is possible to be convicted of one's sins apart from a knowledge of the gospel. He attributes this possibility to the "hidden Christ" who works through the sundry forces of history that drive people to the point of despair.[54] We can infer that the hidden Christ might also work through apologetic discourse (even one that does not contain the kerygma), and therefore apologetics might in some cases be a means of special grace.

It is interesting to compare Niebuhr's view of the relation of apologetics to commitment with Calvin's. Calvin is a kerygmatic theologian who maintains that the gospel and not an apology is the means by which the Holy Spirit brings us faith. According to Calvin the minister should act as the prophets and apostles who "boast not their own genius, or any of those talents which conciliate the faith of the hearers; nor do they insist on arguments from reason."[55] Rather they "bring forward the sacred name of God" which alone can penetrate the hearts of sinners.[56] Calvin believed that once people become Christians, they are then able to confirm their faith by the internal evidences of Scripture and conscience and the external evidences of nature. But Calvin made it clear that these evidences are cogent only for those who are already in the church: "Those persons betray great folly, who wish it to be demonstrated to infidels that the Scripture is the word of God, which cannot be known without faith."[57] Both Niebuhr and Calvin believe that the truth of faith can be validated to a certain degree, but whereas Niebuhr holds that this validation can prepare the way for commitment,

---

[54] *Ibid.*, pp. 109 n., 123.

[55] John Calvin, *Institutes of the Christian Religion*, trans. John Allen, 7th American edition (Philadelphia: Presbyterian Board of Christian Education, 1936), 1, 7, 4:89.

[56] *Ibid.*

[57] *Ibid.*, 1, 8, 13:104.

Calvin maintains that only the gospel can bring about commitment, and the validation of the gospel must necessarily follow commitment.

The difference between Niebuhr and Calvin becomes especially noticeable when we compare their sermons. A close analysis of Niebuhr's sermons reveals that they are not really sermons in the sense of proclamations but rather analytical discourses on the human situation, which can be viewed as preparations for the message. Rather than telling the story of what God has done for us on the cross, Niebuhr concentrates on validating certain insights of the faith, particularly those relating to human sinfulness, by correlating them with established psychological and sociological knowledge. Niebuhr tries to build a case for the Christian religion by demonstrating that we mortals are incapable of understanding ourselves truly apart from certain presuppositions on the nature of humanity and the world that are integral to the Bible but that are also verified daily in human experience. Niebuhr orients his sermons about a text, but he expounds this text primarily in the light of the self-knowledge of contemporary humankind rather than in the light of the biblical message. For example, in his sermon "The Age Between the Ages" Niebuhr takes for his point of departure the third verse of 2 Kings 19: "Thus saith Hezekiah, This day is a day of trouble, and of rebuke, and blasphemy: for the children are come to the birth, and there is not strength to bring forth." (KJV). Rather than relating these words to the New Testament proclamation of the good news of the kingdom that is not of this world, Niebuhr sees these words in the context of the struggle for power on the part of the great nations of the present day. He tries to show on the basis of data gleaned from history and sociology that "all our new births are brought about in pain; and the pain and sorrow of re-birth are greater than the pain of natural birth."[58] He concludes that people today stand in need of the moral resources that Christian faith provides – humility and hope. There is no mention of the events of the cross and resurrection, which comprise the ground of both our

---

[58] *Discerning the Signs of the Times* (New York: Charles Scribner's Sons, 1946), p. 55.

APOLOGETICS AS A MEANS OF VALIDATING THE FAITH 67

hope and humility. In his sermon "The Test of True Prophecy" he makes a psychological analysis of the sources of insecurity in human life and shows that a true prophet is one who does not attempt to ignore or cover up this insecurity in his or her own life.[59] Niebuhr's analysis of the inner turmoils of the self is brilliant, but it must be recognized that this is an exposition of the insecure self, not of the saving acts of God.

In a later sermon "Sorrow and Joy According to the Christian Faith" Niebuhr gives an excellent statement of the nature of Christian joy. A considerable part of this sermon is devoted to showing how "joy" in the biblical sense differs from "happiness" in the philosophical sense.[60] This sermon is especially helpful to a Christian who is striving to understand the faith better, and we must acknowledge that there is a place for sermons that are instructive rather than proclamatory. Yet again it must be seen that this sermon consists not so much in a reiteration of the story of the cross as in an empirical analysis of the self transformed by divine grace.

In his sermon "Zeal Without Knowledge" based on Romans 10:1-13 Niebuhr sets out to verify the biblical insight of the dangers of zeal divorced from the knowledge of God by showing that most of the troubles of the modern world have been caused not by a knowledge divorced from religion but by a "heedless and unwise religion."[61] Niebuhr exposes "zeal without knowledge" in rationalism, romanticism, and Marxism. In this attack upon secular thought, Niebuhr points to Christian faith as a type of zeal that is grounded in true wisdom, wisdom that is validated by the excesses of those who are "wise in their own eyes." Moreover, there is no proclamation of the specific events attested to by the apostles, but only an elucidation of how certain concepts and presuppositions are more tenable and relevant than others.

---

[59] Reinhold Niebuhr, *Beyond Tragedy* (New York: Charles Scribner's Sons, 1937), pp. 89-110.

[60] *Advance*, 145 (July 13, 1953), 5, 6, 27.

[61] *Beyond Tragedy*, p. 229.

Even when Niebuhr expounds such a kerygmatic text as the concluding words of the Apostles' Creed, his sermon is more apologetic than kerygmatic. Rather than telling the story of the resurrection of Christ from the grave and the promise of a general resurrection at the end of time, he tries to show how the idea of the resurrection of the body is more in accord with the highest insights of religion than the rival idea of the immortality of the soul. Niebuhr betrays his ambivalence concerning the sinfulness of humanity when he contends in this sermon that the reason the modern mind rejects the symbols of the Christian hope "lies in its failure to understand the problem of human existence in all its complexity."[62] Rather than confronting his hearers with their idolatry in the light of the crucifixion Niebuhr tries to demonstrate that only the Christian faith provides the key that can help us to understand the multiple facets of human existence.

Calvin's sermons, in contradistinction to Niebuhr's, are not apologies, but proclamations of the message about Jesus Christ. For example, in his sermon on Isaiah 53:4-6, Calvin tries to relate this passage not to secular speculation either in the past or present, but rather to the central affirmations of the New Testament regarding the victory and power of Christ over sin. Calvin demonstrates how each part of the text is related to some specific act of God that is decisive in the purchase of our salvation. He concludes this sermon by calling his hearers to repentance and decision.[63] In his sermon on Isaiah 53:11 he affirms that our righteousness is accomplished in the human nature of Christ, that Christ and not the law is the sole way to salvation, and that faith makes us sharers of the sacrifice of Christ.[64] In his sermon on Isaiah 53:12 he shows how Christ is fully Priest and Mediator, that the death and intercession of Christ are inseparable, that the power of prayer is derived from the sacrifice of Christ, and that all our dignity lies in His intercession.[65] Calvin en-

---

[62] *Ibid.*, p. 306.

[63] John Calvin, *The Gospel According to Isaiah*, trans. Leroy Nixon (Grand Rapids: Eerdmans, 1953), pp. 63-64.

[64] *Ibid.*, pp. 98-115.

[65] *Ibid.*, pp. 116-133.

deavors to interpret the text in the light of the cross rather than in the light of secular patterns of meaning.[66] In his sermon entitled "On the Final Advent of our Lord Jesus Christ" Calvin seeks to correlate the events of the first and second coming of Christ.[67] He bases this elucidation on the inspired insights of the New Testament rather than on a psychological probing into the self-knowledge of the natural person. Rather than demonstrating as Niebuhr does that life in history is incomplete and that the key to this life must lie beyond history, Calvin heralds a specific act of God, viz., the "final advent" and proclaims this act as the content of our hope. His aim is not to validate this event but simply to make it known. Calvin does seek to confirm or support various insights of faith in his theological writings, but these writings are intended only for the community of faith. The sermons are addressed not only to the reborn person but also to the natural person, including the natural person within the Christian.

A word might be said regarding the views of Niebuhr and Calvin on the relation of despair to faith. Like Niebuhr, Calvin holds that despair is directly related to repentance, but unlike Niebuhr, Calvin contends that the despair that is connected with repentance is a concomitant of faith. According to Calvin the only type of despair that leads to repentance is that which the Holy Spirit implants in us when we hear and believe the Word. This is to say that we can know our misery and despair only when we know the crucified Christ.[68] Niebuhr is insistent, on the other hand, that the natural despair brought about by historical circumstances as well as apologetical reasoning is also utilized by the Spirit in bringing people to repentance. Niebuhr sees natural despair as a precon-

---

[66] Calvin would not deny, however, that there is some light in secular thought (due to common grace) and that this light subordinated to the light of the kerygma might illumine certain insights of faith. He differs from Niebuhr in that he does not appeal to the light in secular thought but rather seeks to rechannel this light. He also does not allude to this light in his sermons but only in his dogmatic works.

[67] John Calvin, *The Deity of Christ and Other Sermons*, trans. Leroy Nixon, (Grand Rapids: Eerdmans, 1950), pp. 290-302.

[68] See *Institutes* 3, 3, 7:655-658; 3, 3, 21:673-675; cf. 1, 1, 1-3:47-50. Calvin calls the despair which is connected with repentance "godly sorrow." 3, 3, 7:656.

dition or preparation for the creative despair that prompts people to seek Christ. Therefore Niebuhr sets out to establish contact between the gospel and the despair inherent in life. Calvin does not see apologetical possibilities in natural despair. In his understanding the only type of despair that is saving is that which engulfs alarmed sinners when they are confronted with their guilt in the light of the sacrifice on the cross. Therefore Calvin orients his sermons about the specific events of atonement and redemption (which predicates a declaration of the "law" as well as of the "gospel"). Niebuhr, on the other hand, orients his sermons about the breakdown of self-knowledge, which he believes might well be a means by which our hearers are led into despair, which becomes "creative despair" under the impact of the Holy Spirit.

Karl Barth takes a position that is markedly closer to Calvin than to Niebuhr. With Calvin Barth is adamant that apologetics can in no way bring our hearers to the point of decision. We are made free and willing to decide for Christ only when the message of the cross confronts us in all of its power and glory. Barth acknowledges that the gospel must be supported by evidence, but he says that this evidence is furnished by the gospel itself. It is none other than the assurance of forgiveness and the hope concerning the end. The validation of the faith is given by faith itself; it needs no validation on our part. Barth, like Calvin, believes that in speaking to the world the church must be concerned only to herald the glad tidings of the victory of Christ. Again, like Calvin and also Niebuhr, Barth believes that the truth of faith must be related to other truth, but he insists that this enterprise can be meaningful only within the confines of the church. Barth differs from Calvin in that he does not believe that a reborn reason can validate the faith, although he does say that it can illumine the faith. Both Barth and Calvin stand in opposition to Niebuhr in that they believe that the attempt to support or verify the faith can in no way prepare the way for commitment to this faith. As in the case of Calvin and Niebuhr, the main differences between Barth and Niebuhr become especially pronounced when we compare their sermons. Barth's sermons, unlike Niebuhr's, are oriented almost wholly about the telling of the story about Jesus Christ. Barth, like Calvin, attempts to relate this story to the basic questions of our hearers, but the "basic questions" (in the minds of both these theologians) are not the creative questions of the culture but rather the burning questions about life and death that the Holy Spirit engenders within the repentant sinner.

Niebuhr's principal divergence from the kerygmatic position lies in his approach to people outside the circle of faith. Niebuhr believes that the minister must do something other than simply to preach about "repentance and the remission of sins."[69] He contends that the gospel must be made contemporaneous with the existential situation in which people find themselves. Niebuhr reminds us that the ministers of today are speaking to a particular group of people. They are speaking "to a generation which hoped that historical development would gradually emancipate man from the ambiguity of his position of strength and weakness and would save him from the sin into which he falls by trying to evade or deny the contradiction in which he lives."[70] We must preach in such a way that the mode of salvation that modernity envisages might be shown to be an illusion. This is to say before we try to confront our hearers with their guilt in the light of the cross we must "shake the false islands of security" that they have sought to establish.[71] We must undercut the idolatrous ideology of the secularist before we can proclaim the message "about sin and grace." By undermining the positions of our hearers, we are validating the faith in a negative way, since we are demonstrating the incapacity of reason to solve the enigmas of life. We can also validate the faith in a positive way by showing how the broken insights of culture are fulfilled in revelation. Yet this attempt at validation does not establish the reality of the faith in the minds of our hearers. It only demonstrates the relevance of faith, thereby making it possible for our hearers to make an intelligent commitment.

---

[69] This is how Calvin defined the content of the gospel. See *Institutes* 3, 3, 19:670.

[70] *Faith and History*, p. 243.

[71] *Ibid.*

Niebuhr holds that unless we strive to make the faith relevant to the cultural situation, it will have no persuasiveness and compelling power. It is only when our hearers have been brought to acknowledge the schism in their self-understanding and to experience the anxiety of despair that they will be ready and willing to repent and to receive the forgiveness and saving power of Christ. Only when our hearers have been brought to the boundary of reason which is the "bottomless abyss" will they grasp the hand that can save them. Only then will they surrender to the truth that can make them free. Niebuhr proffers an apologetics that he believes can equip the minister to speak intelligibly and forcefully to the present situation and thereby make it possible for our contemporaries to commit themselves. Whether Niebuhr's approach comports with the revelatory insights of Holy Scripture is the subject of the next chapter.

Chapter V

A Critique of Niebuhr's Methodology

In view of Niebuhr's concern to bring apologetics into accord with biblical truths, I shall undertake in this section to ascertain whether or not the orientation of his apologetics is in fact genuinely biblical. I shall first clarify my own conception of biblical authority and then delineate several guiding principles that I believe are pervasive in the Bible. In the light of these principles I shall proceed to examine Niebuhr's assumptions concerning human nature and the mode of God's saving work. Finally I shall contrast these principles with the apologetic principle.

The Authority of the Bible

It is my thesis that the Bible as a visible historical record has a relative but nevertheless decisive authority for the Christian. This is to say, it is not binding or authoritative in itself, but it points beyond itself to a final authority – the gospel or the message of the cross. The Bible is authoritative not as truth itself but as a witness to truth. It is binding not as an indefeasible criterion but as a formal norm. My basic orientation can therefore be seen to be not too different from Niebuhr's. In dealing with the question of Scriptural authority, I shall consider four basic issues: the inspiration of Scripture, the meaning of revelation, the relation of biblical to ecclesiastical authority and biblical hermeneutics (in the narrow sense).

Niebuhr says little if anything about inspiration, but he does seem to adhere to some kind of inspiration. For example, he contends that people in the Bible "made contact with the divine power," but he does not elaborate on the nature of this contact.[1] He does hold that much in the Bible is contingent and errant. He is not clear, however, as to the precise nature and degree of the contingency in the historical record. Those who have been immersed in the higher criticism of the Bible will readily concur with Niebuhr that there are not only discrepancies of a purely historical nature in the writings but also grave contradictions between the biblical worldview and the findings of modern science. We are even compelled to recognize divergences in theological formulation and in forms of worship within the Bible. What Niebuhr does not point out with sufficient clarity, however, is that within and behind the historical relativity and religio-cultural diversity of the Bible there is an underlying unity of *divine revealing action*, which predicates a unity in *faith-response*. When Niebuhr takes pains to depreciate the faith-response of certain writers, e.g., those who formulated the myth of the Virgin Birth, and then contrasts this response with that of other writers, e.g., those who formulated the myth of the Resurrection,[2] it is legitimate to inquire whether he regards the Bible as inspired in any sense whatsoever.

The inspiration of Scripture has traditionally centered about the problem of how these sacred writings can be considered a product of both God and humanity. Orthodoxy, both in its Protestant and Catholic forms, has taken the Greek word "*theopneustos*" in 2 Tim. 3:16 to signify that kind of verbal inspiration that predicates divine dictation (regarding the written form) and historical and theological inerrancy (regarding the content of the record). Benjamin Warfield held that inspiration means that the Bible as a book or compendium of books "is breathed out by God, 'God-breathed,' the product of the creative breath of God."[3] I would concur with Warfield as over against certain liberals that inspiration means something more than "breathed into" (in the sense of "illumina-

---

[1] *Faith and History*, (New York: Charles Scribner's Sons, 1949), p. 126.
[2] *Ibid.*, p. 148.
[3] Benjamin Warfield, *The Inspiration and Authority of the Bible*, ed. Samuel G. Craig, introduction by Cornelius Van Til (Philadelphia: Presbyterian & Reformed Publishing Co., 1948), p. 133.

tion"). Yet, although Warfield tried to make room for human initiative, he did not succeed in doing justice to the human and fallible character of the biblical writings. He failed to consider the fact that the prophets and apostles of biblical history did not claim to possess an infinite perspective.[4]

I have tried to formulate a doctrine of inspiration in terms of a divine "election" both of the writers and their actual testimony. I conceive of this "election" as a dual process whereby the Spirit of God *guides* the writers in the sense of "opening their eyes" to His self-manifestation in Israelite history culminating in the event of the Incarnation and in addition *preserves* their actual testimony as the special medium of His continual self-disclosure in the community that is founded on the Incarnation. Inspiration does not entail a literal or "naked" knowledge of God in that God infinitely transcends our intramundane forms of thought and intuition; therefore any statement concerning His being and activity must perforce be of a symbolic and analogical nature. Neither does it predicate indefectibility as far as the structured worldview of the biblical writers is concerned. On the other hand, the fact that these writers stood under the direct impact of revelation signifies a certain break in their finite limitations as well as a decisive counteraction of their idolatrous predilections. It is my contention that these men possessed a certain basic understanding of God's will and purpose and that this understanding is sustained by and grounded in the revelation itself (and is by this very fact inerrant). This is not to say that this knowledge is infinite and unlimited, since the Holy Spirit *accommodated* Himself to rather than *abrogated* the cultural environment of the writers. The breadth of this knowledge is determined by the level of revelation to which it corresponds. Again, I maintain that the structured interpretation of the biblical writers, although directed by this revelatory knowledge, was at the same time marred by envi-

---

[4] The writer of 1 Peter pictures the prophets as seeking and striving to understand what the Spirit of the Messiah was teaching them to see (1 Peter 1:10, 11). In the words of the Psalmist: "Such knowledge is too wonderful for me; it is high, I cannot attain it" (Ps. 139:6). Even Jesus is depicted as pointing beyond himself to the "Other", who remains enveloped in mystery (Cf. Matt. 19:17; John 7:16, 17).

ronmental influences (both internal and external) and therefore can at the most be a broken reflection of the content of the Word. Yet even this broken interpretation is normative in so far as it is a product of the paradoxical concurrence of the free will of the writers and the accommodating action of the Spirit. The attestation of the biblical writers differs from that of the "disciples at second hand" (the later Christians) in one important respect: the election or inspiration of these writers necessarily predicates the relative adequacy of their verbal witness to the truth revealed to them.

This brings me to the doctrine of revelation. I conceive of revelation as an incomparable "meeting" between God and the person who comes to believe whereby God speaks and the latter hears. The spoken Word and the human reception together form the revelation or disclosure of God's will and purpose. The "spoken Word" is a metaphor that refers to God's mysterious unveiling of His secret wisdom via human words. Because meaning is not fully grasped until it is structured in verbal form, this symbol appropriately expresses God's revelatory activity. Moreover, revelation has happened in a final and definitive form in the apostolic encounter with Jesus Christ. But this decisive event was not isolated. It presupposes a revelatory history which was a preparation for it and in which it was received. It is this "sacred history" that the biblical writings mirror. Both the expectation of Christ in the Old Testament and the recollection of Christ in the New Testament form an indissoluble part of the revelatory constellation.

The question has perennially been raised as to whether revelation has a determinative content. It has become fashionable in many circles to speak of revelation in terms of an "I-Thou encounter." Yet most contemporary theologians who use this terminology take pains to point out that revelation signifies more than sheer immediacy; it entails knowledge of the significance of this encounter. In the words of the Westminster Confession: "It has pleased God to reveal Himself and to *declare His will* unto the church" (italics mine). I would equate this will with the "law" and the "gospel." Yet I must point out that the law, signifying God's abiding revelation in the history of the Israelites, can be known to be God's will for us only when interpreted in the light of the apostolic kerygma. At the same time, the kerygma itself cannot be rightly understood unless it is seen within the framework of the revelatory history that presupposes it. Again, I must make clear that the law and the gospel as the content of revelation are not to be equated with objective propositions that are at the disposal of natural reason. The Word of God exists for us only when God is actually speaking and we are actually receiving His Word. To borrow Tillich's phrase, the knowledge of revelation is "receiving knowledge," not "controlling knowledge."[5] The Word can be apprehended brokenly, and although it can and must be expressed, it cannot itself be identified with any specific human formulation.

How is revelation related to the Bible as an objective historical record? Although the original human reception of revelation forms an integral part of the revelation itself, this original reception cannot be equated with the objective verbal representation of this reception. The prophets themselves were able to receive this Word of God only through the power of His Spirit in the "Moment of decision." We must pay heed here to Brunner's insightful distinction between "thought-in-encounter" and "thinking-about-it."[6] The objective knowledge that the writers were able to procure in their formulation is at the most an attestation or witness to revelation. This witness is not itself the *Word*, but a human word pointing to the Word which is Jesus Christ. Yet if the biblical writings do not constitute the revelation itself, can they be considered binding upon the Christian? Yes, this objective human record is binding because through the power of the Holy Spirit the words that it contains become "transparent" to their pneumatic meaning, which was received by the writers in the "kairos" event. We must understand the "kairos" event as the "Moment" in which the eternal broke into the temporal and the temporal was empowered to receive it. When this Moment is recreated by the Spirit, the very

---

[5] Paul Tillich, *Systematic Theology*, (Chicago: University of Chicago Press, 1951), 1:97-8.

[6] Emil Brunner, *The Christian Doctrine of God*, trans. Olive Wyon (Philadelphia: Westminster Press, 1950), p. 74.

words in the Bible become the Word of God for us. Revelation "happens" when the *Word* that was spoken to the prophets and the written word are brought together in paradoxical unity.

The subtle relation between revelation and inspiration can now be delineated. Whereas revelation signifies the specific event whereby God's will is unveiled and received, inspiration refers to the divine election of the total human reception of the original revelation (including the verbal representation). Whereas revelation concerns the objective content of God's will and purpose, inspiration refers to the specific human form through which this content is conveyed. The actual statements of the Decalogue might be regarded as "inspired' but they cannot be said to be "revealed." I concur with Niebuhr that it is the error of Protestant scholasticism that it so often equates revelation with the inspired human record. Those who adhere to this orientation fail to grasp the dynamic and inaccessible nature of revelation. Revelation consists not of revealed truths that are objectively "there" in the Bible but of God's special act of condescension whereby His Word is made known to the believing heart.

Since the church fathers canonized the Bible and since this canonization did not take official form until the fourth century A.D., a difficulty arises regarding the relation of biblical to ecclesiastical authority. Roman Catholics maintain that because the Holy Spirit is continuously at work in the Church throughout the ages, the Church is thereby invested with the authority to determine which books are binding upon Christians. If those who vindicate ecclesiastical over biblical authority would consider Tillich's distinction between original and dependent revelation,[7] the problem might be seen in a clearer light. Original revelation consists in the original twofold act of divine condescension and human reception. Revelation that occurs outside of this original constellation is "dependent" in the sense that it is bound to the original reception (and indirectly to the original interpretation). This is what Calvin meant when he averred that the Spirit freely binds Himself to the Word

---

[7] See Paul Tillich, *Systematic Theology*, 1:126.

(i.e., the biblical testimony). The Church therefore cannot authorize the canon, but simply certify or recognize it. The problem of why these books are to be canonized and no others has of course not been resolved. I simply contend that the providential preservation and aggrandizement of the canonical writings forms an integral part of the "election" of these writings. Because in the last analysis it is the Holy Spirit who authorizes the books of the Bible, we cannot argue absolutely for a closed canon. Here I would take issue with John Knox who in his *Criticism and Faith* argues for the closed canon on the basis that only the authorized sacred writings stand in immediate historical proximity with the Christ revelation.[8] Yet what about certain apocryphal books such as First and Second Maccabbees which might very well have been chronologically closer to the miracle of the Incarnation than some of the New Testament writings? In answering this question Knox might be compelled to come to a conclusion not very different from mine: it is not historical but "superhistorical" proximity to the original act of unveiling that determines canonicity. "Superhistorical" proximity entails not only the historical proximity of the writings, but also the revelatory potentiality of their message. This, of course, is another way of stating that the canon is correlative with the speaking of the Spirit. This speaking, moreover, must not be understood as a creation of new truth, but as a *reiteration* of truth that has already been disclosed once for all. At the same time (since this speaking encounters us in the Bible), it is a *confirmation* of the intrinsic faithfulness of the biblical attestation to this truth. The criterion of "superhistorical" proximity tends to rule out the apocrypha, but it does not rule out possible undiscovered writings that may have been preserved by the Spirit for aggrandizement at a future time. Although we do not have the power to fix the boundaries of the canon in any absolute sense, the canon is closed in a limited or relative sense, in so far as any addition can be made only when the Christian community as a

---

[8] See John Knox, *Criticism and Faith* (New York: Abingdon-Cokesbury Press, 1952), pp. 66-69.

whole is directly moved toward this act by the overwhelming power of the Holy Spirit.

I have already touched on many facets of the hermeneutical problem, but I shall now proceed to address this problem in general. In the medieval period four meanings were to be sought in every text: the literal, the allegorical, the moral, and the mystical. The Reformers rightly protested against this approach, since it opened the door to arbitrary exegesis. I concur with the Reformers that one must search for the literal (signifying here the original) meaning in every Scripture text. This literal meaning, however, cannot be uncovered by a simple translation. The literal sense is one that is found in the original text when its component words are understood in the light of the worldview and the scale of values of the author. But after the literal meaning is uncovered, biblical hermeneutics does not end. Historical exegesis must be supplemented by theological exegesis. This means that we must now try to relate the total theological and axiological insights of the writer to the center or apex of biblical history – the event of Jesus Christ. Such an undertaking is outside the confines of higher criticism. Only the believer who is guided by the Holy Spirit can discern the subtle relation of the insights of the writer to the revelation of the Son of Man. This relation unveils the innermost intentions of the writer, intentions of which he himself might not have been completely aware.[9] Historical exegesis gives us the literal sense of the biblical passage, i.e., what the writer *actually said* in terms of the cultural imagery of his day. Theological exegesis (which in the case of the Old Testament writings may take the form of typological exposition) discloses what the writer was *trying to say*. It uncovers the *telos* (inner meaning) that directs the imaginative predilections of the writer and that finds its culmination in God's decisive action in Jesus Christ.

Biblical interpretation might be regarded as a fourfold process. First one must approach the Bible with a certain degree of fear

---

[9] As one prophet testifies: "I have uttered what I did not understand, things too wonderful for me, which I did not know." Job 42: 3; Cf. Dan. 12:8.

and reverence inasmuch as it is a "sacred object" of the tradition. This presupposes that the reader is a believer, one who is seeking for the truth revealed by God. Yet the pre-critical must give way to a critical stage in which the reader subjects these sacred writings to scientific scrutiny. Because of the biblical warning against absolutizing the relative, the reader by trying to penetrate behind the outward imagery is simply remaining true to the demands of faith. The reader who accepts the Bible uncritically will inevitably convert the Bible into a heteronomous authority or "idol." But objective or scientific criticism must in turn be superseded by a "criticism turned inwards" or what might better be termed "radical doubt." We are now not only critical of the Bible as a finite object, but also of ourselves, of our own presuppositions and ideological predilections. Indeed, if we take our historical relativity and existential estrangement seriously, we will finally be compelled to doubt (and therefore overthrow) every norm or criterion of metaphysical import that is arrived at by natural reason. It is then that we will see the relevance of Calvin's admonition: "We must be emptied of our own understanding in order to have a saving knowledge of God" (paraphrase).[10] It is at this point that radical doubt or criticism pushed to the limit gives way to prayer. After acknowledging that we cannot find God, we must call on God to find us. It is in this Moment of despair that the Holy God discloses His will and favor toward us. It is then that the human hermeneutical enterprise is transmuted into a divine enterprise. The Bible is now its own interpreter. This Moment of revelation does not simply obfuscate or annihilate our rational capacities. Indeed, it would be more correct to say that it converts our reason or directs our reason back to the center of faith. Without this meeting with the mind of Christ the historical critic is at a loss to uncover the kerygmatic import of any specific Scripture text. Under the power of this revelation the ordinary person who is truly critical of his or her own insights and worthiness in the sight of God can know this secret wisdom before the secular historical

---

[10] John Calvin, *Commentary on the Epistles of Paul the Apostle to the Corinthians*, 1 Cor. 1:21, trans. John Pringle (Edinburgh: Calvin Translation Society, 1848), 1:84.

scholar. To be sure, the scholar (if a believer) will be more able to apprehend the overall significance of the faith of the Bible, but this difference is one of degree, not of kind.

Niebuhr's hermeneutics appears to be very similar to the one I have just delineated, although there are certain basic differences. Against orthodoxy he attempts to interpret the Bible in the light of the kerygma rather than in the light of certain time-bound confessions. He contends that only through an encounter with the "mind of Christ" can we uncover the full significance of any specific biblical text.[11] Yet Niebuhr does not sufficiently connect this encounter with a knowledge of the objective biblical record. He holds that one can come to experience the reality of Christ apart from an appropriation of the original meaning of the Scripture text, even apart from a knowledge of the historical Jesus.[12] He does not fully discern that we hear the "Word" only in and through the objective "word" of the Bible. The "Word" does not negate or suspend the meaning of the Scripture text but rather illumines and clarifies this meaning. Both Luther and Calvin censured the mystics and sectarians for tending to divorce the experience of the Spirit from the letter of the Bible.[13]

Methodological Principles

On the basis of the revelation contained in Holy Scripture, it is possible to construct a theological methodology.[14] This methodology is not, of course, a divine methodology and is therefore subject to criticism in the light of the Biblical message. Yet I hold that it is relatively consistent with the basic affirmations of the Bible and

---

[11] Reinhold Niebuhr, "An Answer to Karl Barth," *The Christian Century*, 66, no. 8 (Feb. 23, 1949), p. 235.

[12] *Supra*, pp.64-65.

[13] Luther denounced the spiritualists and enthusiasts as visionaries (*Schwärmerei*).

[14] By "methodology" I mean the set of principles that guide one in the interpretation of the data of any given area of experience. Methodology might therefore be defined as a "theory of truth" or a "systematic path to knowledge." A theological methodology signifies the prolegomenon to theology.

can therefore guide us in the evaluation of Reinhold Niebuhr's apologetics.

The first methodological principle is what Kierkegaard terms "the infinite qualitative difference" between the divine and the human or the eternal and the temporal. This difference is cogently stated by the prophet Isaiah in the Old Testament: "My thoughts are not your thoughts, neither are your ways my ways, says the Lord. For as the heavens are higher than the earth, so are my ways higher than your ways and my thoughts than your thoughts."[15] Paul reaffirms this insight by describing God's judgments as "unsearchable" and his ways "inscrutable."[16] This same viewpoint is found in 1 Timothy where it is written that God "has immortality and dwells in unapproachable light, whom no man has ever seen or can see."[17] The discontinuity between God and humanity is also stressed in the wisdom literature of the Old Testament, although this insight is partially blurred in the optimism of Proverbs. The contention of the writer of Ecclesiastes that "God is in heaven and man upon earth" was the central affirmation of the early Barthian school.[18] The writer of Job says regarding the wisdom of God: "It is hid from the eyes of all living, and concealed from the birds of the air."[19] Even in Proverbs one can find statements that are analogous to those that I have cited.[20]

The infinite difference between God and humanity is not caused by finitude in the first instance, since God has bridged the barrier of finitude by means of general revelation. The abyss that separates God and humanity comes from our side: it has its source in human sin. This insight is found in the first chapters of Genesis and throughout the Old Testament. It is present in the synoptic Gospels, but it is nowhere more clearly enunciated than in the first

---

[15] Isa. 55: 8,9.
[16] Rom. 11:33.
[17] 1 Tim. 6: 16.
[18] Eccl. 5:2.
[19] Job 28:21.
[20] Cf. Prov. 3:5; 28:25, 26.

chapter of Romans. Paul contends that ever since the creation of the world the invisible nature of God "has been clearly perceived in the things that have been made."[21] Yet because of our idolatrous arrogance our minds have become "darkened" and our thinking "futile."[22] Claiming to be wise, people "became fools, and exchanged the glory of the immortal God for images resembling mortal man or birds or animals or reptiles."[23] Because of the revelation in creation the barrier between God and mortals is not absolute. Because of human sin, however, there can be no saving knowledge of God apart from His special revelation.

It is my contention that sin infects every part of the human being. In our sin we may well yearn for God, but we have been rendered incapable of seeking God. We may well stand in need of the grace of God, but our will has become bound to the driving power of sin, and our reason has become blinded to the truth that can free us. The difference between God and humankind is therefore irrevocable and insurmountable as far as human resources are concerned. I shall try to show in the next section how Scripture further confirms the doctrine of total depravity.

My second methodological principle is that God can be known only by means of His self-disclosure in Jesus Christ. As Jesus is reported to have said: "No one knows the Father except the Son and any one to whom the Son chooses to reveal him."[24] Put another way, this means that God can be known only in and through Himself. Because mortals are separated from God by sin, they cannot find God through their own power. If God is to be known, God must give Himself to be known. God must bridge the barrier of sin, and He has done this in the person of Jesus Christ. Revelation is an event in which God not only incarnates His Word in human flesh but also creates within the human subject the faculty to apprehend His Word. Apart from this twofold miracle, we would remain en-

---

[21] Rom. 1.20.
[22] Rom. 1:21.
[23] Rom. 1:22, 23.
[24] Matt. 11:27; Cf. John 1: 9-13; 14:6; Rom. 8:1-11; 1 John 4:7-9.

compassed in darkness. Karl Barth puts this very succinctly: "There is *no* way which leads to this event; there is *no* faculty in man for apprehending it; for the way and the faculty are themselves new, being the revelation and faith, the knowing and being known enjoyed by the new man."[25]

We must now consider in what sense we can regard the Word or revelation of God as a criterion for knowledge. If the Word is not at our disposal, how can we criticize our own thinking and also the thinking of others in the light of the Word? I contend that the Word of God illumines and transforms our reason thereby enabling us to subject various viewpoints to His scrutiny. Because the Word is the criterion of as well as the judgment on all meaning, we can through the power of the Word discern the antinomies as well as the valid insights in secular and also Christian thought. Because, as Niebuhr says, the Word contains within Himself the key to the "whole of history,"[26] we can through His power partially unravel the enigmas of history. Yet we must remember that because the Word is not a category of reason (although Niebuhr at times seems to think otherwise)[27] but rather an act of God that illumines and at the same time stands over against the categories, we cannot exhaust the Word in any rational formulation. Indeed, every statement that we make concerning the Word is subject to criticism by the Word and therefore provisional. The absolute standpoint remains the possession of God, and our statements as well as our ideas of this standpoint must be necessarily self-negating and self-transcending. Yet because the Word of God Himself directs and transforms our reasoning process, we can be fairly certain which ideas and standpoints point or lead to the absolute. Under the guidance of the Word we can also be certain which structures of meaning contravene or obscure the absolute. Because the Word of God is not only the ground of meaning but also the goal of mean-

---

[25] Karl Barth, *The Word of God and the Word of Man*, trans. Douglas Horton (Chicago: Pilgrim Press, 1928), p. 197.

[26] *Faith and History*, p. 141.

[27] See *Human Nature*, p. 143.

ing, we have the assurance that our broken knowledge of the Word will be fulfilled "beyond history." Then the insurmountable barrier between God and humanity will have been surmounted. My epistemology therefore can be seen to have an eschatological orientation. This orientation is acutely expressed by the apostle: "For now we see in a mirror dimly, but then face to face. Now I know in part; then I shall understand fully, even as I have been fully understood."[28]

My third methodological principle is that the content of revelation cannot be divorced from its mythical form in the act of meaningful communication. By the mythical form I mean the inner form of the biblical language (not to be confused with the dialect or outer form). The mythical form is synonymous with what Barth calls the "language of Canaan." The contemporary demythologizing controversy has brought this problem into sharp focus. I would tend to side with Barth and to a lesser extent Niebuhr[29] as over against Bultmann that the meaning of the gospel cannot be extricated from its mythical form without losing the force of this meaning. If myth is defined as a description of divine activity in this-worldly terms, then myth is the only possible form of expression that can portray God's unfathomable incursion into the history mirrored in the Bible. Again, if meaning conditions language from within, as many linguists maintain, then the meaning of the gospel, which is the ground and negation of all other meaning, can be possessed only in the mystery of its own peculiar worldliness. This is another way of stating that the Bible myth is inspired or that the Bible myth has been elected by God as the visible means of His self-manifestation.

Does this mean that we cannot interpret the myth in any way? In opposition to a certain kind of naïve fundamentalism I believe that the myth must be recognized for what it is and therefore

---

[28] 1 Cor. 13:12. For Niebuhr's cogent assimilation of this insight see *Faith and History*, p. 214.

[29] Niebuhr would seem to agree that only the biblical myth can adequately express the truth of faith, but he would tend to deny that the Holy Spirit freely binds Himself to this myth.

must be interpreted. In contradistinction to existentialist theology I believe that the authentic interpretation must allow for the determinative role of the myth in the communication of the gospel. One can interpret the myth by ascertaining its immediate historical context, its parallels in the surrounding culture, and its peculiar significance in the faith of the covenantal community. On the basis of such an analysis one can make certain literal statements regarding the historical structure of the myth, i.e., whether it is a pictorial recording of an historical fact, a pictorial explanation of an historical fact, or a pictorial depiction of a truth that universally characterizes humanity's relationship with God. One can also make certain literal statements of a negative nature, which entails making clear what the myth does *not* mean and (in the case of myths referring to historical events) making clear what did *not* happen. The only positive statements we can make regarding the content of the myth will be of an analogical character and will necessarily become a part of the "language of Canaan." This is to say that the innermost meaning of the myth can be expressed only in terms of the myth itself, which signifies that the gospel forever remains concealed from natural reason. Indeed, because the Word of God and the self-understanding of the natural person stand in irreconcilable contradiction, the Church must simply submit to the Word in obedient confession, for it is the Word Himself who creates the necessary "point of contact" that enables the person in sin to make a faithful response. This is not to deny that God works in fallen humans despite and even against their basic predilections and that the theologian can therefore incorporate certain cultural and philosophical insights. At the same time, I aver that those symbols from culture that are taken over by the Church will invariably be "baptized" or "transformed" and thereby subsumed under the primal symbols of the Bible. Any movement toward saving truth in secular philosophy is accidental and can be rightly appreciated only when seen in the light of the sacred history mirrored in the Bible myth.

My guiding principles can be seen to be similar to but yet quite different from Niebuhr's. I concur with Niebuhr that human beings are separated from God because of sin, but Niebuhr would not regard this separation as "infinite" or "insurmountable." Indeed, Niebuhr would indubitably repudiate my first principle as being more Platonic than Christian.[30] He maintains that the natural person can know very much about God, even that God is righteous and merciful. I claim that God is known only through His self-disclosure in Jesus Christ, which brings to sinful humans the power as well as the reality of faith. Niebuhr believes that we can do something to prepare the way for faith in Christ. While I believe that the event of salvation is effected solely from the side of God, Niebuhr sees this event as having both a divine and a human pole. I hold that God does not make His Word known apart from its inspired mythical form. This is to say that I believe that the actual testimony contained in the Bible is the divinely appointed means of grace or means of faith. The basis of faith is the Incarnate Word, but the channel through which He encounters us is the inspired word of the prophets and apostles. Niebuhr regards the biblical myth as important but not as decisive for our salvation. He holds that it is possible to be convicted of sin and to be liberated by grace apart from a knowledge of the biblical testimony, even that concerning the person of Christ.[31]

In the following two sections I shall proceed to appraise Niebuhr's methodology in the light of what I consider to be a biblical methodology. Because my methodology predicates the inspiration of the biblical writers, my appeal will be to the insights of these writers. At the same time, my methodological principles will be further explicated and confirmed.[32]

---

[30] *Reflections On the End of An Era* (New York: Charles Scribner's Sons, 1934), pp. 286 ff.

[31] *Supra*, pp. 64-65.

[32] I have stated thus far only those methodological principles that I believe will be helpful in evaluating Niebuhr's theology. Other principles, such as the work of common grace in the fallen world, will be mentioned in the final chapter where I will try to see apologetics in a new light.

Niebuhr's Anthropology

Niebuhr upholds the grandeur of humanity on the grounds that we are created in the image of God and also the misery of humanity on the grounds that we have sinfully misused our God-given powers. I believe that Niebuhr locates human grandeur too much in our native capacities for seeking and finding truth. The Bible appears to find the grandeur of humanity in the human role in the plan of salvation. I also hold that Niebuhr centers human misery too much in the inevitability of sin and not enough in the eviscerating consequences of sin. To be sure, Niebuhr gives a remarkably astute portrayal of the disruptive power of sin in people's lives, but he does not, in my judgment, do justice to the extent of this disruption.[33] Niebuhr posits an "original righteousness" the effects of which persist in humanity despite sin. And he holds that because of this original righteousness the natural person is in quest of God and is also free to respond to God. As I see it, this position appears to contravene the biblical principle of the infinite qualitative gulf between God and humanity and also the correlative biblical principle that God can be known only through Himself.

Niebuhr is quite emphatic that the natural person is in search of God: "The fact of self-transcendence leads inevitably to the search for a God who transcends the world."[34] He qualifies this proposition in that he acknowledges that apart from the grace of God this search will culminate in idolatry. He believes that in many

---

[33] I take exception to Niebuhr's view concerning the extent of the disruption caused by sin, but I find his doctrine of the origin of sin to be very penetrating. Yet in this connection there remain certain questions that I would like to see Niebuhr elucidate further. For example, Niebuhr holds that the same freedom which tempts to anxiety "also contains the ideal possibility of knowing God" (*Human Nature*, p. 252). He hopes in this way to safeguard the belief that mortals are to be held responsible for their sin. Yet it is difficult to know what Niebuhr means by "ideal possibility." At times he seems to hold that this is a possibility which is reached when human free-will is fulfilled by grace. I hold that grace does not fulfill our inherent freedom but brings us a new freedom. From my viewpoint the "ideal possibility" can only refer to a state of being that might have been possible had not sin entered the world.

[34] *Human Nature*, p. 165.

cases the native quest for God is perverted into a quest for glory and happiness."[35] Yet he is convinced that it is possible for the natural person to "strain after" and to seek the unconditional.[36] Our seeking must be partially negated before we can embrace the truth of the gospel, but this seeking is nevertheless real. It is especially important for apologetics, since it provides the "point of contact" between the gospel and the world.[37] In this particular context he speaks of "yearning" rather than "seeking," but from what he says in other places it can be seen that he links the two very closely. Indeed, if our wills did not actually seek revelation, our yearnings for revelation would provide no point of contact. On the whole Niebuhr's view is strikingly similar to that of Augustine who envisaged salvation as the fulfillment of a quest or an ascent to heaven made possible by grace. Fallen humans seek for God, but they are unable to reach God apart from God's condescension in Jesus Christ. Niebuhr says: "Religion is, on the one hand, a moral adventure, a climb of 'the steep ascent to heaven,' and on the other hand a dispensation of grace by which heaven descends to those who can never reach it."[38]

In opposition to Niebuhr I believe that on the basis of a faithful reading of the biblical testimony the human will cannot be regarded as being congruent with God's will or even directed toward God's will. In the third chapter of Genesis we are told that Adam after his sin seeks to hide from God.[39] He is ashamed and also afraid to face God, because he is faintly aware of the fact that he stands guilty in the sight of God. His heart might long or yearn

---

[35] Niebuhr does not go as far as Tillich who says: "Reason does not resist revelation. It asks for revelation, for revelation means the reintegration of reason." *Systematic Theology*, 1:94.

[36] *Reflections On the End of An Era*, p. 114.

[37] "Coherence, Incoherence, and Christian Faith" in *Christian Realism and Political Problems*, (New York: Charles Scribner's Sons, 1953), p. 196.

[38] Reinhold Niebuhr, "Christianity and Redemption" in *Whither Christianity*, ed. Lynn Harold Hough (New York: Harper and Brothers, 1929), p. 121.

[39] Gen. 3:8.

for revelation, but his will seeks to escape from revelation.[40] I consider this passage typical and representative of the biblical witness concerning the human drama. We would not be sufficiently critical if we ignored the many passages in which humans are represented as seeking God. Yet I believe it can be shown that the context of such passages either implies or explicitly states that those persons have already been found by God. The Reformers rightly interpreted such verses as meaning that the Spirit of God within redeemed humanity is seeking the truth of faith; the old nature, even the old nature within the Christian, always strives to escape from this truth.[41] There is, of course, the natural quest for meaning and security which the biblical writers would not deny, but they would affirm that this natural quest is not really a search for God, even though it might be called that, and they would tend to deny that there is any point of contact between this type of quest and the Christian answer. Niebuhr, on the other hand, sees in this quest a means through which God works and which the apologist can appeal to in order to bring people in sin to the "boundary situation," thereby preparing them for the message of deliverance.

In order to show how my methodological principles are reflected in the biblical witness, I shall proceed to give a critical interpretation of Jeremiah 29:13, which appears to support Niebuhr's contention that humanity seeks God. This is to be regarded not as an exhaustive exegesis but rather as an examination of a specific verse in the light of its immediate theological context. The writer says: "You will seek me and find me; when you seek me with all your heart, I will be found by you." These are the words of a letter that the prophet Jeremiah sent to the Jewish people in Babylon, who several years before had been carried away into exile by the Chaldeans. In this letter Jeremiah reminds the people that it was

---

[40] Niebuhr is aware that sinful humanity tries to hide from God, but he interprets this dialectically. Humans not only try to hide from God but they also try to find God.

[41] The extent of the perversion of human reason is admirably expressed by Calvin: "Human reason...neither approaches, nor tends, nor directs its view towards this truth, to understand who is the true God, or in what character he will manifest himself to us." *Institutes of the Christian Religion*, trans. John Allen, 7th American edition (Philadelphia: Presbyterian Board of Christian Education, 1936), 2, 2, 18:299.

God who sent them into exile. He admonishes them not to be deceived by any prophet who predicts a speedy restoration. He writes to the exiles that they must adapt themselves to their new environment and work for the welfare of the city in which they find themselves. He says that they will be permitted to return to their homeland only when they seek Yahweh with their whole heart. In the concluding section of his letter Jeremiah predicts divine retribution upon those Jews who have remained in Jerusalem and who pursue their own idolatrous desires rather than God' will.

Jeremiah's interpretation of history must be seen against the background of his understanding of the nature of God. Jeremiah conceived of God as both holy and almighty. He had a profound appreciation for the providential rule of God over all of history. This providential rule does not preclude human freedom if by freedom is meant the power to act as one desires to act. Yet the prophet seems to believe that humans through their rebellion against God have lost the desire or motivation to turn toward God.[42] This loss of God-ward motivation is regarded in itself as an act of God whereby God vents His wrath upon His rebellious subjects. God, being a holy God, is pictured as being especially hostile toward hypocrisy. This is why God is said to use peoples who are explicitly pagan in order to chastise and humble His own people who give lip service to His law, but who in reality seek to live apart from His law.

Since Jeremiah seems to regard rebellious humanity as incapable of turning toward God, why then does he write to the exiles and call upon them to seek God? We must first of all recognize that Jeremiah is pointing to an event that is conceived as being brought about by the special providential activity of God. Human beings are viewed as being able to seek God not because they are believed to possess any inherent capacity for seeking truth but because God is acting in and through them. In verse 10 the writer speaks of God as promising to "visit" His people in their exile. God is depicted as saying: "I will fulfill to you my promise and bring you back to this

---

[42] Cf. Jer. 6:10; 9:5, 6; 13:23.

place. For I know the plans I have for you...plans for welfare and not for evil, to give you a future and a hope."[43] After God reveals that He will confront His people in this special way He is represented as saying in verse 12: "*Then* you will call upon me and come and pray to me, and I will hear you" (italics mine). The exiles will begin to seek God, because God is seeking them. They will find God, because God is acting in and through them in order to bring them back to their homeland.

Those who try to find in Jeremiah 29:13 and similar verses the biblical authority to posit an inherent human capacity for seeking and finding the truth of revelation are apparently ignoring the deeper meaning patterns within the Bible. I hold that on this basis humans can be regarded as seeking God but that this possibility is bestowed on them by God. It does not reside within sinful humanity as such. Therefore there can be an appeal not to the original righteousness of humanity but only to the righteousness and wisdom of God.

Another verse that might be construed as supporting Niebuhr's position is Romans 7:18b: "I can will what is right, but I cannot do it." If Paul is speaking as a person under the law, and not as a Christian, then one can infer that human beings seek the good, even though they cannot achieve their goal. There is cogent evidence (on the basis of verse 25b and also on the basis of similar passages in other epistles) to support the view that Paul is describing his present inner conflict. My intention is not to give a critical analysis of the verse under discussion but rather to point to various interpretations that illustrate the tension between the two types of theology. Niebuhr seems to take the position that Paul does speak as a person under the law.[44] This position is also held by other apologetic theologians, including Origen, Tillich, Bultmann, and Brunner. One reason why they take this stand is their concern to safeguard the freedom of the Christian. At the same time they im-

---

[43] Jer. 29:10, 11.

[44] Cf. *Discerning the Signs of the Times*, (New York: Charles Scribner's Sons, 1946), p. 163; *Reflections On the End of An Era*, p. 114; *Human Destiny*, p. 292.

ply, even though this might not be their intention, that the natural person at least seeks for the good and the true. Calvin together with such theologians as Luther and Nygren, who might be classified as "kerygmatic," holds that Paul is speaking as a Christian, not as a person under the law. Calvin, more than the others, bases his argument on the presupposition that the natural person is incapable of willing or seeking the good.

> Those who attribute it to the first grace of God, that we are able to will effectually, seem...to imply that the soul has a faculty of spontaneously aspiring to what is good, but that it is too weak to rise into a solid affection, or to excite any endeavour. And there is no doubt that the schoolmen have in general embraced this opinion, which was borrowed from Origen and some of the fathers, since they frequently consider man in things purely natural, as they express themselves, according to the description given by the Apostle in these words: "The good that I would, I do not; but the evil which I would not, that I do. To will is present with me; but how to perform that which is good, I find not." But this is a miserable and complete perversion of the argument which Paul is pursuing in that passage. For he is treating of the Christian conflict, which he more briefly hints at to the Galatians; the conflict which the faithful perpetually experience within themselves in the contention between the flesh and the spirit.[45]

Niebuhr not only does not adequately recognize the paralyzing effect of sin upon the direction of the human will, but he also does not seem to see the bearing of this effect upon the freedom of the will. Niebuhr holds that because of general revelation people "are able to entertain the more precise revelations of the character and purpose of God."[46] He rejects the view that the sinful human being is "blind to the possibilities of a disclosure of the Eternal which transcends him."[47] He contends that in the present age there

---

[45] Calvin, *Institutes*, 2, 2, 27:309.

[46] *Human Nature*, p. 127.

[47] *Human Destiny*, p. 38.

is a "receptivity" toward the message of the Bible.[48] He portrays the gospel as a "live option" for today thereby implying that it is possible for the person in sin to believe.[49] He acknowledges that this person is not totally free to appropriate the truth of faith. Yet he is convinced that we are free to recognize the forces that limit our freedom and also the saving power that can fulfill our freedom. Niebuhr's position is essentially synergistic. Fallen humans are able to recognize and to respond to Christ because of common grace. Yet apart from the power of Christ they are unable to complete this response because of original sin. Niebuhr had already arrived at this general position at an early time. He says in his autobiography: "There is enough natural grace in the human heart to respond to the challenge of the real message in the gospel – and enough original sin in human nature to create opposition to it."[50]

I hold that the person in sin cannot be regarded as free to decide for God because of the qualitative abyss between human knowledge and predilections and the mind of God, an abyss that has its source in humanity's idolatrous desire to be God. This insight I believe to be in accordance with the overall biblical testimony. The prophets and apostles generally picture human beings as having lost the freedom to save themselves through rebellion. On the basis of their own power they are unable not only to find their way back to God but also to respond when God finds them. Sin not only blinds their vision but also shackles their will. When the biblical writers speak of humanity as being lost, they have more in mind than the fact that humans have strayed away from the fold: they mean that humans find themselves as prisoners in another fold. By following their own desires rather than God's will, they have become slaves to their desires. They do not surrender themselves to the God who can liberate them because they are unable to

---

[48] Reinhold Niebuhr, "Is There A Revival in Religion?" *New York Times Magazine*, Sect. 6 (Nov. 19, 1950), p. 13.

[49] Reinhold Niebuhr, "The Tide of Religious Faith", *The Messenger*, 20 (May 3, 1955), p. 7.

[50] Reinhold Niebuhr, *Leaves from the Notebook of a Tamed Cynic* (Chicago: Willet, Clark, & Colby, 1929), p. 41.

do so. To be sure, there are passages that picture humans as being free to respond to God, but here again, the context of such passages generally indicates that such people have already been confronted by God and have thereby been granted new knowledge and new power.

The parable of the sower might be cited by Niebuhr and others who sympathize with the apologetic enterprise in its traditional form as establishing the inherent freedom of humanity to accept or reject the gospel. I shall proceed to give a critical interpretation of the Markan version of the parable, since this version furnishes the basis for the statements of the parable in Matthew and Luke.[51]

It must be acknowledged that Mark appears to support Niebuhr's allegation that the human person is capable of hearing and believing the gospel. The parable proves to be a parable not of the sower, but rather of types of soil – the types of people to whom the gospel is addressed. The sower goes out to sow, but only the seeds that fall on the good soil bring forth grain. The seeds that fall on the path are devoured by the birds; the seeds that fall on the rocky ground have no depth of soil and wither away under the scorching heat of the sun. The seeds that fall among the thorns grow but are choked by the thorns before they can yield grain. Mark concludes the first section of the parable in these words: "He who has ears to hear, let him hear."[52] On the basis of this verse one commentator says that it is "strongly suggested…that men could *choose* to hear and respond."[53]

In the explanation of the parable, however, we are given what would appear to be a slightly different understanding of God's knowability (see particularly verses 10-13). This explanation might possibly be a later addition to the original record, but this does not detract from its relevance to the question at hand, since it reflects the apostolic interpretation of the parable, an interpretation that is

---

[51] Mark 4:4-20.

[52] Mark 4:9.

[53] Frederick C. Grant, Introduction and Exegesis of Mark in *Interpreter's Bible* (New York: Abingdon, 1951), 7:698.

present in the other Synoptic Gospels. In verse 11 it is suggested that those who believe have been given a special power to believe by God. The writer pictures Jesus as saying to his disciples: "To you has been given the secret of the kingdom of God, but for those outside everything is in parables; so that they may indeed see but not perceive, and may indeed hear but not understand; lest they should turn again, and be forgiven."[54] The meaning is not that the parables are intended to confuse, but that they will inevitably confuse those whose minds have not been illumined by grace. It is not until we have been transformed into "good soil" that the Word can be appropriated. The Word must therefore be viewed as a secret wisdom in that it is known only by the beneficiaries of grace. According to Frederick Grant this interpretation represents a perversion of the original meaning of the parable and was motivated by the twin perils of worldliness and persecution that occurred at the time Mark was written and that tended to thwart the growth of the church.[55] I must point out, however, that worldliness and antagonism towards the gospel were also present at the time of Jesus and that Jesus Himself emphasizes the incapacity of humans apart from grace to know God.[56]

When one compares the Markan version of the parable with the versions in the other Gospels, particularly Matthew, the view is reinforced that the believing heart is itself a special creation of God. The writer of the Gospel of Matthew gives added emphasis to the verses in Isaiah 6 which draw a distinction between hearing and understanding, seeing and perceiving. The writer suggests that those whom the herald addresses might very well hear the sounds of his words, but not imbibe their inner meaning. The reason is that the receptivity of the natural person has been dulled and obfuscated by sin. There appears to be some receptivity on the part of sinful humanity, but this receptivity proves to be deceptive, since there is no real appropriation of the truth of faith. Regarding those who do

---

[54] Mark 4:11-12.

[55] *Interpreter's Bible*, 7:695-702.

[56] Cf. Matt. 11:25-27; Mark 10:23-27.

respond our Lord says: "Blessed are your eyes, for they see, and your ears, for they hear," thereby implying that authentic hearing and seeing are a divine blessing.[57] This insight does not detract from the view that the human person is responsible for making a free decision for Christ. It tends to exclude the other view, however, that this freedom is natural and inherent in humanity.

Niebuhr is concerned to safeguard the paradox of divine election and human free decision, and therefore he stresses our native freedom to answer the command of God.[58] According to Niebuhr God takes the initiative, but we as God's creation have the power to respond. Yet one must ask whether the paradox can be interpreted in this manner. To be sure, a person coming to faith makes a free decision for Christ, but is not this freedom a gift of special grace rather than a native endowment? We have the capacity to say "Yes" to the gospel of Christ, but I hold that this capacity is not inherent but rather is created within us by the gospel itself. The paradox is that the free decision is a part of the divine election. The writer of Acts says: "As many as were ordained to eternal life believed."[59] This is the mystery of the gospel, a mystery that cannot be resolved in synergism.

Moreover, I hold that Niebuhr does not adequately appreciate the blinding effects of sin upon reason in that he is betrayed at times into regarding the Word of God as being amenable to rational appropriation. I must qualify this criticism, however, in the light of the fact that he continually stresses the mystery of the Word. Niebuhr reveals his Enlightenment lineage when he refers to the truth of revelation as a "category" or "presupposition" and

---

[57] Matt. 13:16.

[58] Niebuhr states the paradox in the following manner: "From the level of the sinful self, surveying its own situation, it is always true that it has the possibility of, and therefore responsibility for, becoming conscious of the undue character of its self-love. But when the self stands beyond itself 'by faith,' it is conscious of the fact that nothing it has done or can do is free of debt to the miracle of grace." *Human Destiny*, p. 118. The context of this statement indicates that the self's free response is completed and fulfilled by grace rather than created by grace.

[59] Acts 13:48.

compares this truth to other categories and presuppositions.[60] He often subsumes the Christian position within a typology, thereby reducing it to a philosophical position. It must be admitted that Niebuhr is aware of the dangers in this approach:

> There is a peril in this way of interpreting the Gospel truth. The peril lies in the tendency to reduce Christianity to yet another philosophy, profounder than other philosophies because it embodies heights and depths which are not comprehended in the others.[61]

To his credit it must be said that perhaps more than any other theologian Niebuhr strives to hold mystery and meaning together in paradoxical tension. Against the mystics he avers that the testimony of the Bible is more than poetry; against the rationalists he holds that this testimony cannot be rendered explicable by a philosophy.[62] Although the biblical testimony has pronounced metaphysical implications and therefore can lend itself to the criticism of metaphysical systems, this testimony itself is not a metaphysics. Niebuhr points out that because the prophets and apostles are describing events that transcend the outer limits of reason, they are compelled to utilize mythical and paradoxical language. There is enough meaning that shines through the myths and paradoxes to enable the theologian to relate the truth of faith to other truths. Niebuhr holds, however, that this relation will be symbolic and not univocal. In contradistinction to Tillich he tends to give a more determinative content to the "symbol" by conceiving it more in terms of an analogy than of a metaphor.[63] Yet Niebuhr seems to take away some of the mystery of faith by claiming that this analogical relation between the truth of faith and other truths can be discerned by natural reason. This is the doctrine of the *analogia entis* which has always been prominent in apologetic theology. In place of the *analogia entis* I suggest the *analogia fidei* which means

---

[60] Cf. *Human Nature*, pp. 12, 129-130, 143.

[61] "Coherence, Incoherence, and the Christian Faith" in *Christian Realism and Political Problems*, p 198.

[62] See Niebuhr, *Discerning the Signs of the Times*, pp. 171-73.

[63] For the difference see *supra*, pp. 41-42.

that the analogical relation can be discerned only by the new person, i.e., on the basis of faith.[64]

In summary, I hold that Niebuhr fails to discern the full dimensions of the helplessness and lostness of humanity. In order to do justice to the grandeur of humanity, he posits special capacities within us for seeking and apprehending the truth of God. He does not seem to see that our grandeur consists not so much in what we can do as in what God does for and through us. In positing these special capacities Niebuhr appears to lose sight of the abysmal difference between God and humanity, a difference that must be understood in terms of a contradiction between our thinking and willing and the Word of God. In alleging that there is an inherent human possibility for knowing God, Niebuhr also does not do justice to the biblical principle that God can be known only through Himself, i.e., only through His Holy Spirit as this transforming influence comes to us from the cross of Christ. He does not see that because human cognitive powers are blinded and obfuscated by sin, we can be saved only when these powers are miraculously transformed and created anew by grace. Because he does not always grasp the radical depths of sin, he does not fully appreciate the radical nature of grace.

Niebuhr on the Means of Grace

Niebuhr's doctrine of original righteousness must be supplemented by his doctrine of grace if we are to understand his apologetics fully. For Niebuhr it is not enough for humans to be able to seek and respond to revelation. The Holy Spirit must work through our seeking and the questions that arise from this seeking if we are to be brought into a saving relationship with God. I have already alluded to the synergistic character of his doctrine of grace in the last section. In this section I shall concentrate on his conception of the mode of the operation of grace. It is Niebuhr's steadfast conviction that an apology is one of the basic means through which the

---

[64] *Supra*, p. 43.

Holy Spirit works (whether this be in the direct sense of securing conviction or in the indirect sense of preparing the way for conviction). Niebuhr opposes the traditional view that the Word and the sacraments are the only appointed means of grace. He holds that a sophisticated attack upon the viewpoint of the adversary can also be a channel through which the Holy Spirit brings that person to decision. He contends that a Christian life is another instrument of the Holy Spirit. In one essay he avers that it is wrong to preach about the second advent, since this message appears fantastic to the modern mind. Instead, we should emphasize a "life of soberness and watchfulness...which will appeal to a world in the night of despair as having some gleams of light in it."[65]

It can be seen that Niebuhr's view contradicts my guiding principle that the divinely appointed channel of redemption is the biblical myth or story concerning this redemption. I believe that this principle is supported by the biblical testimony. The theology or theologies of the New Testament speak only of the heralding of the story of the cross as a means of grace. In the eyes of the New Testament Christians should base their appeal not on the wisdom of the world, but rather on the folly of the gospel. This point of view is cogently stated by Paul: "Since, in the wisdom of God, the world did not know God through wisdom, it pleased God through the folly of what we preach to save those who believe."[66] The New Testament does imply that there are derivative means of grace such as a Christian life and the sacraments, but these are regarded as contingent upon the preaching and hearing of the biblical word. Apologetical reasoning cannot even be viewed as a derivative means of grace if we are to take the New Testament as our authority.[67]

Niebuhr alludes to Paul's address to the people of Athens as recorded in Acts 17 in support of his view that an apology might be

---

[65] Reinhold Niebuhr, "Christ the Hope of the World," *Religion In Life*, 23, no. 3 (Summer, 1954), p. 340.

[66] 1 Cor. 1:21; cf. 2 Cor. 5:20.

[67] It must be borne in mind that some apologies contain sermons, i.e., statements of the story about God's atoning action on the cross, and therefore can indirectly be a means through which the Holy Spirit brings us faith.

regarded as the means by which the Spirit moves a person toward a decision.[68] It is to be acknowledged that this passage appears to provide formidable support for Niebuhr's position and therefore warrants critical consideration.

It cannot be denied that Paul in his address at Athens appeals not to the folly of the cross but rather to the wisdom of his hearers. He was undoubtedly motivated in this approach by a desire to respond to the criticism leveled against him by the Athenian intellectuals.[69] Paul begins his address by commending the religiosity of his hearers. He then speaks about their altar erected to an "unknown god": "What therefore you worship as unknown, this I proclaim to you."[70] He tells them that the God who made the world cannot be contained in the shrines made by humans. He then speaks about the universality of God and the omnipresence of God. He says that since we are the offspring of God, we must not think that God is like anything that mortals can create or even imagine. Paul concludes his address by announcing that God has fixed a day on which to judge the world and that the hope of the world is to be found in a man whom God raised from the dead. When the people hear about the resurrection, many mock, but others manifest some interest. What is significant is that Paul endeavors to bring the religious strivings of his hearers and the message about Christ into conjunction or even correlation. He tries to build a bridge between the ideology of these pagans (especially Stoicism) and the gospel. In this attempt it can be seen that he minimizes if he does not ignore completely the scandal of the cross. His address is to be regarded not as a sermon, in the sense I have defined it, but rather as an apology.

Although one must recognize that Paul utilized the apologetic approach in Athens, biblical scholars almost invariably agree that Paul's mission in Athens was a failure. There is no record of

---

[68] "Coherence, Incoherence, and Christian Faith" in *Christian Realism and Political Problems*, p. 196.

[69] Acts 17:18-20.

[70] Acts 17:23.

any church being established after Paul's visit. Paul himself refers to the household of Stephanas in Corinth and not to the Athenians as the "first converts in Achaia."[71] Paul seems to have been aware of this failure almost immediately after his address for when he reached Corinth which was next on his itinerary, he professed to know nothing "except Jesus Christ and him crucified."[72] He continually asserts in his letters to the Corinthians that the preaching about the crucified Christ is the appointed means of grace. He insists that the telling of the biblical story is the channel through which the Holy Spirit wills to bring to people the power of salvation.[73]

One must raise the question why there is this apparent discrepancy between Paul's approach in Athens and in Corinth. It has been suggested that perhaps Luke, the acknowledged author of Acts, misinterpreted Paul. Because of Paul's very pointed attack upon the apologetic approach in Corinth, I believe that there is more justification for postulating a growth in theological understanding in Paul. Whatever be the case, I believe that Paul's apologetic address in Athens cannot be cited as an example of biblical support for viewing an apology as a means of grace, since Paul himself explicitly inveighs against this kind of approach and affirms in almost all his letters that the Spirit of God freely binds Himself to the proclamation of the kerygma.

The Protestant Reformers vigorously reaffirmed what I believe to be the biblical position regarding the means of grace. Luther says: "We never read that the Holy Spirit was given to any one when he did works, but always when men have heard the Gospel of Christ and the mercy of God."[74] "For we must first hear the Word, and then afterwards the Holy Ghost works in our hearts; he works in the hearts of whom he will, and how he will, but never without

---

[71] 1 Cor. 16.15.

[72] 1 Cor. 2:2.

[73] Cf. 1 Cor. 1:21-23; 2:1-4, 10-15; 2 Cor. 5:20.

[74] Martin Luther, "Treatise on Good Works" in *Works of Martin Luther*, trans. W.A. Lambert (Philadelphia: A.J. Holman Co., 1915), 1:204.

the Word."[75] Calvin also regards the gospel as the special medium of the Holy Spirit: "The word is as necessary to faith, as the living root of the tree is to the fruit; because...none can trust in God but those who know his name."[76] Yet at one place Calvin asserts that God is not bound by necessity to the heralding of the Word:

> They do not consider, that when the apostle makes hearing the source of faith, he only describes the ordinary economy and dispensation of the Lord, which he generally observes in the calling of his people; but does not prescribe a perpetual rule for him, precluding his employment of any other method; which he has certainly employed in the calling of many, to whom he has given the true knowledge of himself in an internal manner, by the illumination of his Spirit, without the intervention of any preaching.[77]

Calvin in a rare moment admits the possibility of faith apart from preaching, but this is by the internal illumination of the Spirit. He nowhere speaks of an apologia as a means of grace; in fact he excludes this type of reasoning as a channel of the Holy Spirit.[78]

It is interesting to note that Niebuhr's position on the means of grace has more affinity with the Protestant scholastics than with the Reformers. Both Lutheran and Calvinist scholastics departed from the kerygmatic basis of the Reformation by conceiving of apologetic reasoning as a channel of divine grace, whether this be in terms of primary or preparatory grace. Rather than allowing God to vindicate Himself in the preaching of the Word, the supposed defenders of orthodoxy have sought to help God by persuading the unbeliever of the reasonableness of the faith. Melanchthon deviated from the Reformation position by conceiving of philosophy as a propaedeutic device that leads one to the sermon.[79] Warfield con-

---

[75] Martin Luther, *The Table Talk of Martin Luther*, ed. with introduction by Thomas S. Kepler (New York: World, 1952), p. 143.

[76] Calvin, *Institutes*, 3, 2, 31:632.

[77] Calvin, *Institutes*, 4, 16, 19:621-22.

[78] *Supra*, pp. 65-71.

[79] For an admirable survey of attempts of Lutheran scholastics to prove the faith see Jaroslav Pelikan, *From Luther to Kierkegaard* (St. Louis, Mo.: Concordia, 1950), pp. 24-75.

tends that the peculiar medium of the Spirit is the "indicia" or the arguments for the divinity of Scripture. He supposedly states Calvin's position, but actually he subverts this position.[80] According to Carnell "logic can be the means by which the Spirit leads a man into faith."[81] Van Til holds that just as the grace of God gives the human person the ability to perceive the truth in preaching "so it is also the Spirit of God that must give man the ability to accept the truth as it is presented to him in apologetical reasoning."[82] Machen states this general position very cogently:

> Of course a man never was won to Christ *merely* by argument. That is perfectly clear. There must be the mysterious work of the Spirit of God in the new birth. Without that, all our arguments are quite useless. But because argument is insufficient, it does not follow that it is unnecessary. What the Holy Spirit does in the new birth is not to make a man a Christian regardless of the evidence, but on the contrary to clear away the mists from his eyes and enable him to attend to the evidence.[83]

A corollary of Niebuhr's view regarding the channels of grace is his universalism. By conceiving of a hidden Christ who operates everywhere in history and through all types of means, Niebuhr affirms that all people are given the possibility of salvation. This can especially be seen in his criticism of Augustine's equation of the "two cities" with two kinds of people on the grounds that the saving love of God encompasses all mortals.[84] Niebuhr also implies that the possibility of salvation will be converted into an actuality if not in this life then beyond history. The Bible tends to be particu-

---

[80] For a trenchant criticism of Warfield on this point see Edward A. Dowey, Jr., *The Knowledge of God in Calvin's Theology* (New York: Columbia University Press, 1952), pp. 115, 116.

[81] Edward John Carnell, *An Introduction to Christian Apologetics*, second edition (Grand Rapids, Mich.: Eerdmans, 1948), p. 70.

[82] Cornelius Van Til, "Introduction" in Benjamin Warfield, *The Inspiration and Authority of the Bible*, p. 39.

[83] J. Gresham Machen, *The Christian Faith in the Modern World* (New York: Macmillan, 1936), p. 63.

[84] Reinhold Niebuhr, "Augustine's Political Realism" in *Christian Realism and Political Problems*, p. 138.

laristic rather than universalistic. Although there are passages especially in Paul's letters that can be interpreted as supporting universalism, these passages are counterbalanced by an exclusivistic conception of the means of grace. It would not be unScriptural to maintain that the general New Testament position is that Christ elects only those who believe and the extent of the number of the elect is not disclosed with any finality. Niebuhr's position is not very dissimilar from Tillich's conception of the latent church, which is intended to include all those who are not in the manifest or historic church. In this view the church is not a saved remnant called out of the world for service and sacrifice, but rather the world as such.[85]

The Apologetic Principle

I have defined the apologetic principle as that which assumes the possibility of common ground between the meaning-orientations of human beings and divine revelation.[86] This principle is basic to Niebuhr's theology. Apart from this supposition much of Niebuhr's underlying approach would be abrogated.

In the light of Holy Scripture it can be argued that the apologetic principle is a product of human speculation rather than revelatory insight. I have sought to demonstrate on the basis of Scripture that there is an irreconcilable contradiction between human hopes and aspirations and the Word of God. I have shown on the basis of Scripture that the natural person can neither apprehend nor respond to the Word of God. Because sin has perverted our will and blinded our reason, we are totally lost and irremediably confused apart from an act of divine grace. Niebuhr declares, "As long as there is...a point of contact there is something in man to which

---

[85] For Tillich's most recent statement regarding the latent church see Paul Tillich, "The Theology of Missions," *Christianity and Crisis*, 15, no. 5 (April 4, 1955), pp. 35-38. Tillich maintains that that which is latent must become manifest, thereby indicating that the manifest church will ultimately include the sum total of the human race.

[86] *Supra*, pp. 35-38.

appeal can be made."[87] But there is no point of contact between the human nous and the divine logos that has epistemological significance, and consequently there can be no appeal to the structure of meaning held by the natural person. The appeal must be solely to the Word of God, who alone can break down the barrier of sin and create a new self.

Niebuhr is acutely aware of the discrepancies between the insights of the Bible and much of the apologetic theology of the past. He is alert to the dangers of syncretizing the biblical message and the ideology of the culture. At the same time, he rightly perceives the perils of isolating the message from the meaning-patterns of the culture. He tries to relate the Word of God and the cultural world of meaning in a paradoxical manner. According to Niebuhr the Word both fulfills and negates this world of meaning. It signifies the answer that the person in sin seeks but never finds. It contains within itself the solution that the natural person is dimly aware of but can never truly know.

What Niebuhr fails to perceive is that the very attempt to convince the unbeliever of the validity of the faith signifies a merging of the Word and secular currents of meaning. This attempt involves a watering down of the radical nature of sin. It predicates the substituting of a criterion held in common with secular thought for the Word of God. Moreover, it places the emphasis of theology on the persuasion of the mind rather than on the heralding of a message. Niebuhr is surely right in his insistence that the message must be related to the culture. But he does not fully discern that this relation between the Bible and culture can only be vertical as over against dialectical. This is to say that there can be no mutual give and take between the Word and culture; the Word must be considered the sole source of meaning and the culture the recipient of meaning.[88] Because there is no point of connection between the sin-tainted patterns of meaning of the culture and the Word of God,

---

[87] *Human Destiny*, p. 117.

[88] It must be pointed out, however, that the meaning which the Word bestows on culture in turn illumines the meaning of the Word.

the Word can be our only point of departure. In other words, we must try to see the human situation in the light of the Word rather than in the transitory lights of the culture if we are to see it correctly.

Niebuhr is betrayed into affirming the apologetic principle by assimilating too uncritically the insights of the Renaissance. He himself acknowledges that his theology represents a synthesis of the Renaissance and Reformation rather than a repristination of the Reformation position.[89] The scholars of the Renaissance were noted for their emphasis on the freedom and indeterminate possibilities of humanity. The Reformers stressed the limitations and captivity of humanity. Niebuhr contends that the Reformers went too far in their interpretation of the binding power of sin and thereby failed to do justice to humanity's inherent capacities. They particularly failed to give a satisfactory account of people's native capacity to recognize their limitations and bondage. It is well to note that Niebuhr holds that the Renaissance and Reformation reflect two correlative emphases within the Bible. His attempt to unite the two movements must therefore be viewed as an effort to remain true to the revelatory insights of Scripture. It is my contention, however, that the Reformers' analyses of these insights, particularly those relating to the corrupting power of sin, are on the whole, more true to the biblical world of meaning than are Niebuhr's.

The guiding principle of Niebuhr's methodology is that there is a connecting link between the inner world of the Bible and the secular world. He finds the possibility of this connection in general revelation and its concomitant original righteousness. Niebuhr has an acute understanding of the disrupting work of sin, but he sometimes creates the impression that sin does not seriously impair the epistemological efficacy of the connecting link. Niebuhr's basic appeal is to the Bible, and his conception of the authority of the Bible is not very different from mine. Yet he has served to diminish this authority by appealing also to the insights of culture, and his speculation has in the process become severed from its kerygmatic

---

[89] *Ibid.*, pp. 207-208.

ground. A recent interpreter of Niebuhr contends that Niebuhr succeeds in relating his analytic approach to a synthetic or kerygmatic perspective, but from what has been said in this chapter I must take issue with this interpreter.[90]

On the basis of the Bible I have proffered several guiding principles that stand in opposition to the guiding principle or principles of apologetic theology. The first is that there is an infinite qualitative difference between divinity and humanity, one that reflects humanity's incapacity to seek and know God. The second is that God can be known only through His Word, i.e., only through Himself. This implies that God is self-justifying and self-authenticating. The third is that God has elected the inspired testimony of Scripture as the primary or ordinary channel of His revelation. I have not tried to ignore the findings of the higher criticism of the Bible; at the same time I have arrived at my conception of the authority of the Bible on the basis of knowledge that is not dependent on historical and textual criticism. Neither have I sought to isolate the message of the Bible from the cultural panorama. I have tried only to guard against any type of synthesis with the ideology of the culture, a synthesis that I believe Niebuhr, despite his very penetrating criticisms of syncretic theology, does not eschew. In the final chapter I shall try to show how the biblical message can be related in a positive way to the meaning-patterns of the culture, but this relation will be one-sided rather than dialectical, i.e., it will proceed from the message to the situation rather than being in the form of an interplay between the two. I shall also try to formulate a new role for apologetics, but it will be an apologetics grounded in the principles of a kerygmatic theology rather than in what I have denominated as the "apologetic principle." My constructive statement will entail a further evaluation of Niebuhr's methodology particularly as this concerns his conception of the validation of the faith.

---

[90] See Hans Hofmann, *The Theology of Reinhold Niebuhr*, trans. Louise Pettibone Smith (New York: Charles Scribner's Sons, 1956), pp. 242-245.

Chapter VI

A New Role for Apologetics

The Mission of the Church

In this chapter I will try to reevaluate the role of apologetics within the context of the mission or purpose of the church. Holy Scripture tells us that the mission of the church is to uphold or glorify God before the world. In the words of the Psalmist: "You who fear the Lord, praise him! all you sons of Jacob, glorify him, and stand in awe of him, all you sons of Israel!"[1] Paul reaffirms this theme: "May the God of steadfastness and encouragement grant you to live in such harmony with one another, in accord with Christ Jesus, that together you may with one voice glorify the God and Father of our Lord Jesus Christ."[2] The fundamental mission of the church is neither to convert people nor to satisfy their spiritual needs, though we can hope that through our preaching many will be converted and fulfilled in God's own time and way. The church must not be preeminently concerned with humanity at all or even with itself. The church as a creation of God must fix its vision upon God, for it is from Him that it receives its life and power.

We are told that the church glorifies God by confessing what He has done for us in the person of Jesus Christ. Paul says: "You will glorify God by your obedience in acknowledging the gospel of Christ."[3] This confession is primarily a verbal confession, but it is also one of deed. As Jesus says: "Let your light so shine before men, that they may see your good works and give glory to your Father

---

[1] Ps. 22:23; Cf. 1 Chr. 16:23-34.
[2] Rom. 15: 5, 6.
[3] 2 Cor. 9:13.

who is in heaven."[4] The more formal type of action that Christ commanded and that comprises the cultus of the church is the sacrament. A sacrament might be defined as an ordinance instituted by Christ Himself in which by visible signs and means He imparts and preserves the new life. The two sacraments testified to in the Bible are Holy Baptism and the Lord's Supper.[5]

Despite the fact that a true confession will always involve both words and actions, the primary medium is the word. Because we cannot really know something until we have structured it in words, faith and the proclamation of faith are inextricably bound together. Good works will always flow from faith, but we first have to have the faith, and we do not have it until we have confessed it by word of mouth. It is for this reason that I conceive testifying to be the primary means of confession and therefore also the primary means of grace. The sacramental act and a Christian life can be regarded as means of confession and grace only in a derivative or contingent sense.

Jesus Himself stressed testifying or the verbal confession of faith: "Every one who acknowledges me before men, I also will acknowledge before my Father who is in heaven."[6] When the demoniac who was healed by Jesus begged to go with him, Jesus said: "Return to your home, and *declare* how much God has done for you" (italics mine).[7] When one of his followers desired to bury his father, Jesus said: "Leave the dead to bury their own dead; but as for you, go and *proclaim* the kingdom of God" (italics mine).[8] One writer records Jesus' command to his disciples after his resurrection in the following words: "Go into all the world and *preach* the gospel to the whole creation" (italics mine).[9] Another writer records it in a slightly different way: "You shall receive power when the Holy

---

[4] Matt. 5:16.

[5] Cf. Matt. 28: 18-20; Matt. 26: 26-28; Mark 14: 22-24; Luke 22: 19, 20; 1 Cor. 11: 23-25.

[6] Matt. 10:32.

[7] Luke 8:39.

[8] Luke 9:60.

[9] Mark 16:15.

Spirit has come upon you; and you shall be my *witnesses* in Jerusalem and in all Judea and Samaria and to the end of the earth" (italics mine).[10]

The apostle Paul also emphasized the decisive role of testifying: "If you confess with your lips that Jesus is Lord and believe in your heart that God raised him from the dead, you will be saved."[11] And again: "It pleased God through the folly of what we preach to save those who believe."[12] Paul regarded the sacraments as important, but there is reason to believe that he did not consider them indispensable for salvation: "For Christ did not send me to baptize but to preach the gospel, and not with eloquent wisdom, lest the cross of Christ be emptied of its power."[13]

The biblical writers tell us that God is glorified whenever we proclaim His Word, but they also admonish us to make certain that what we proclaim is His Word and not something else. To state this in a different way, it is not enough just to speak certain words: we must understand the meaning and impact of these words on both the writers and our hearers. In order to understand this meaningfully, we must know the historical situation in which these words were originally uttered, the various theological interpretations of these words throughout history (including heretical interpretations), and also the use or misuse of these words in those circles outside the church. In other words, in order to witness intelligibly, particularly in a public setting, we must have a working knowledge not only of biblical and historical theology but also of secular philosophy, both ancient and modern. It is in this latter area that the apologetic concern belongs. I shall speak more of this in the succeeding sections of this chapter.

In the task of confessing the faith intelligibly, we must remember that our purpose in doing so is not to placate our hearers

---

[10] Acts 1:8.

[11] Rom. 10:9.

[12] 1 Cor. 1:21; cf. Rom. 10:17.

[13] 1 Cor. 1:17.

but to please God.[14] We must make certain that we understand the faith and also the situation, but we do this only so that we can better proclaim the folly of the cross. Since God is glorified through the heralding of the evangel, it is our responsibility to build our theology upon the evangel, not upon the wisdom of the world. Moreover, since God the Holy Spirit has designated the evangel as the means by which He wills to build His church, the Christian can do no more than to trust and obey the evangel. If the church arrogates to itself the power to convert, then it has abandoned its purpose of glorifying God for that of aggrandizing itself. Whenever the church tries to build itself up rather than serve the Son of Man, the Holy Spirit will abandon the church to the fate that claims every other historical institution. The church can survive as a vehicle of salvation only if it confesses Jesus Christ as its Master and Lord. It is from Christ alone that it derives its power and vitality. If the church once severs itself from the ground of its being, it will either disintegrate or become dominated by the prevailing ideology of the surrounding culture.

It was because the Reformers believed that the church had forsaken its mission that they desired to reform or purify the church. Calvin excoriated the priests of the church: "They invite none to faith in Christ and a faithful participation of the sacraments; but rather for purposes of gain bring forward their own work instead of the grace and merit of Christ."[15] The Reformers went so far as to claim that there is no church apart from the confession and adoration of Jesus Christ. Calvin asserted "first, that the Church may exist without any visible form; secondly, that its form is not contained in that external splendour which they foolishly admire, but is distinguished by a very different criterion, *viz.*, the pure preaching of God's word, and the legitimate administration of the sacraments."[16] And in the words of Luther: "Wherefore, the

---

[14] Cf. Gal. 1:10.

[15] Calvin, "Dedication," *Institutes of the Christian Religion*, trans. John Allen, 7th American edition (Philadelphia: Presbyterian Board of Christian Education, 1936), 1: 30.

[16] *Ibid.*, p. 33.

Church is holy even where fantastical spirits do reign, if only they deny not the Word and Sacraments. For if these be denied, there cannot be the Church."[17]

Niebuhr would indubitably agree that the basic purpose of the church is to uphold the Word of reconciliation before the world, but he would diverge from my position regarding the nature of this confession. At one place he says: "We must...preach the gospel to this, as to every generation. Our gospel is one which assures salvation in the Cross of Christ to those who heartily repent of their sins."[18] Yet Niebuhr goes on to insist out that "the Cross is a revelation of the love of God only to those who have first stood under it as a judgment."[19] At another place he declares: "Evangelical Christianity...desires, so to confront the soul with Christ, that as Judge he would drive the old self to despair and that as Redeemer he would transmute despair into repentance."[20] Apart from the context of these statements it would appear that Niebuhr speaks as an evangelical theologian, but his emphasis on the negative approach has tended to divert his attention from the biblical story of God's saving acts. Where Niebuhr departs from the evangelical position is that rather than envisaging the confession of the cross as a reiteration of the story of the cross, he sees this confession more as an attempt on the part of ministers to undercut or expose the false centers of meaning of their hearers and thereby to bring them to the abyss or outer limits of reason. I concur with Niebuhr that the sermon must always include a word of judgment, but is not this word an indictment of our sin in the light of the cross rather than an exposure of the contradictions and ambiguities in our speculation? Because Niebuhr concentrates more on demonstrating the untenability of the presuppositions of modern skeptics than on confronting them with their tragic participation in the crucifixion

---

[17] Martin Luther, *A Commentary on St. Paul's Epistle to the Galatians*, trans. Philip S. Watson (London: James Clarke & Co., 1953), p. 40.

[18] *Christianity and Power Politics*, (New York: Charles Scribner's Sons, 1940), p. 210.

[19] *Ibid*.

[20] Reinhold Niebuhr, "A Problem of Evangelical Christianity," *Christianity and Crisis*, 6, no. 8 (May 13, 1946), p. 5.

and the hope of the resurrection, he tends to orient his witness more about criteria held in common with secular thought than about the Word of God. For the most part his approach is patterned along the lines of the traditional attack and defense rather than proclamation. His method consists more in proffering or presenting a set of concepts that are deemed more adequate than other concepts or presuppositions and that are regarded as amenable to rational appropriation rather than pointing to or witnessing to an event or series of events in the past.[21] This is why Niebuhr's theology is more apologetic than kerygmatic in the sense that I am using these terms. He does not fully appreciate the fact that because human reason is blinded by sin, there can be no appeal to the meaning-orientations held by the person in sin, even though this appeal is motivated by a desire to overthrow these meaning-orientations. It follows that there can be no proper apology in the traditional sense of the word.[22] The theologian can appeal only to the Word of God who has chosen to speak not through an apology but rather through the kerygma and allow the Word to build His kingdom in His own way and in His own time. As Calvin says: "God does not now rule otherwise in the world than by his gospel; nor is his maj-

---

[21] In the case of some of the younger theologians who have been influenced by Niebuhr there is a marked tendency to stress the symbols of the faith as over against the objective events upon which the faith is founded. This gnostic tendency can especially be seen in Charles D. Kean, *The Meaning of Existence* (New York: Harper & Brothers, 1947).

[22] Despite the fact that an apology cannot properly convey the faith to its hearers, something that has often been called an "apology" is permissible under certain circumstances. The writer of 1 Peter says: "Always be prepared to make a defense to any one who calls you to account for the hope that is in you" (3:15). This is to say that if people come to us raising questions about our faith, we should try to answer their questions. Our purpose in such action, however, is not to convert our questioners but rather not to offend them unnecessarily. Through such action we might be able to gain some insight into their background so that we can speak about the gospel in terms familiar to them. Again, it is permissible to vindicate the church as an institution, especially if it is under attack. Our purpose, here, is again not to convert our hearers, but rather to convince them of our right to exist and proselytize. Since an apology in its true sense signifies the attempt to defend the faith with the purpose of winning converts, the foregoing attempts cannot properly be spoken of as apologies but only as statements of conviction.

esty otherwise rightly honoured but when it is adored as known from his word."[23]

Faith Seeking Understanding

The mission of the church is to witness to the miracle of the Incarnation; yet this entails much more than the mere act of preaching. I have already indicated that it is important for the church to witness intelligibly, and this predicates faith seeking understanding. Paul writes to the Corinthians: "I hope you will understand fully, as you have understood in part."[24] The writer of 1 Peter portrays the prophets as searching and inquiring after their faith.[25] This is to say that it is not enough to have faith; we must seek to understand our faith. Only in this way can we make sure that we are communicating the kerygma and not some ideology. Moreover, in seeking to understand our faith we are thereby enabled to know God more intimately. We consequently grow in the grace and favor of God.

The need of the church to understand the faith in order to witness more effectively has brought into being kerygmatic theology. Kerygmatic theology has for its aim the explication of Holy Scripture within the church and before the world. This explication within the church entails instruction in the fundamentals of the faith as well as the vindication of the faith against heresy. As one apostle says, the minister "must hold firm to the sure word as taught, so that he may be able to give instruction in sound doctrine and also to confute those who contradict it."[26] In order to fulfill its aim kerygmatic theology calls for a scrutiny of the original languages of the Bible, the history of ancient culture, church history, historical theology, practical disciplines and the history of philoso-

---

[23] Calvin, *Commentaries on the Epistle of Paul the Apostle to the Romans*, trans. and ed. John Owen (Edinburgh: Calvin Translation Society, 1849), p. 502.

[24] 2 Cor. 1: 13, 14.

[25] 1 Peter 1:10.

[26] Titus 1:9.

phy.[27] I include the history of philosophy not only because we cannot truly understand the heresies that emerge within the church until we know something of their sources in the secular realm, but also because we cannot understand the message fully until we see it in the light of attacks both from within the church and from the world.

This concern within kerygmatic theology for understanding and combating secular philosophy is the apologetic concern seen in its rightful place. It is a concern to answer attacks upon the faith from the world outside the church, but primarily for the purpose of helping the Christian to understand the claims of faith more adequately. The traditional apologetic concern of seeking to overthrow the position of unbelievers in order to bring them to the gospel has little place in the church. I envisage the apologetic concern as part of the general kerygmatic concern or what Barth would call the "dogmatic" concern. There is a place for an apologetics that serves the mandate of witnessing but not one that constitutes a strategy of defense. The mission of the church is to witness to the faith for the glory of God. But in order to witness effectively we must understand the truth of faith, and to understand this truth adequately we must wrestle with attacks upon this truth from outside the church. A certain type of apologetics has a valid place within the church so long as its purpose is to help Christians understand their faith better, not to make this faith respectable in the eyes of the world. This is to say, the church should be engaged in the scrutiny of secular thought not so much in order to convince secularists of their errors and thereby to compel them to accept the gospel, but rather to understand its commission better. As Barth says: "The Church must enter into the questions and movements of the age, but in order, by

---

[27] In one sense kerygmatic theology entails interaction with nearly every conceivable discipline. Because we are impelled to interpret the whole of experience in the light of our faith, even the natural sciences are thereby brought under the domain of theology. Our primary aim in seeking to know more about the world and the life of the world is to know more about the goodness of God (whether this be in the form of creation or redemption) so that we can better praise and glorify Him.

so doing, to understand anew and to understand better what the true Church is."[28]

At this point a word might be in order on how human reason is capable of understanding the content of faith. I have said previously that the truth of faith is inaccessible to reason, primarily because our reason has been disrupted by sin. Sin has shattered the basic continuity between God and humanity, but I must stress the fact that it has not destroyed this continuity entirely. Indeed, if this rupture were total, then the human person would be completely isolated from God and would at once disintegrate into nothingness. There is still a formal ontological relation between God and sinful humanity, although this relation has no epistemological significance. In other words there remains after sin a formal point of contact between the Word of God and human reason, but no material point of contact. This is to say that although there is a point of contact between the Word and the basic structure of human reason, there is no possibility of integration between the Word and the perverted direction of human reasoning. The natural person, because of sin, is incapable of both hearing and believing the Word, but is not isolated from the Word entirely.

It is my contention that when we participate in the body of Christ which is incarnate in the church, our whole being, including our reason, is thereby healed and transformed. Through the power of God the "imago Dei" is restored or created anew. The perverted direction of our reasoning is counteracted, and our reason is now united with its source and ground. The revelation of God does not destroy reason but rather liberates reason from its bondage to the driving power of sin. The basic ontological relation between the Word and the creation can now be discerned and appreciated. Because we participate in the body of Christ only in discontinuous moments of decision, our transformation is only partial, yet it is nevertheless real. I concur with Niebuhr that the ideological taint remains in the thinking of the Christian, but I contend that this taint is in the process of being eradicated by the Holy Spirit. St.

---

[28] Barth, *Against the Stream*, (London: SCM Press, 1954) pp. 228, 229.

Paul cogently analyzes the work of reason when it is grounded in the power of the Holy Spirit:

> So also no one comprehends the thoughts of God except the Spirit of God. Now we have received not the spirit of the world, but the Spirit which is from God, that we might understand the gifts bestowed on us by God. And we impart this in words not taught by human wisdom but taught by the Spirit, interpreting spiritual truths to those who possess the Spirit.[29]

This illumination of human reason by revelation was nowhere better understood than by Luther. This Reformer often denounced reason as an enemy of the faith. Yet the context of such statements indicates that he was thinking of natural reason or the reason of the old nature, not sanctified reason or the reason of the reborn nature. He had only praise for reasoning that is centered or grounded in the revelation of Christ.

> The natural wisdom of a human creature in matters of faith, until he be regenerate and born anew, is altogether darkness, knowing nothing in divine cases. But in a faithful person, regenerate and enlightened by the Holy Spirit, through the Word, it is a fair and glorious instrument, and work of God: for even as all God's gifts, natural instruments, and expert faculties, are hurtful to the ungodly, even so are they wholesome and saving to the good and godly.[30]

And again:

> The understanding, through faith, receives life from faith; that which was dead, is made alive again; like as our bodies, in [the] light day, when it is clear and bright, are better disposed, rise, move, walk, etc., more readily and safely than they do in the dark night, so it is with human reason, which strives not against faith, when enlightened, but rather furthers and advances it.[31]

---

[29] 1 Cor. 2: 11-13.

[30] *The Table Talk of Martin Luther*, ed. with introduction by Thomas S. Kepler (New York: World, 1952), p. 181.

[31] *Ibid.*, pp. 181, 182.

Luther suggests in this last sentence that an enlightened reason can not only amplify the truth of faith but also strengthen faith. Indeed, when we seek to understand the world about us in the light of this truth, our faith will become more firm and more alive. At the same time, there always remains the possibility of losing the power of faith if we let our preoccupation with the theological superstructure divert our vision from the ground of our faith. Once we turn away from the ground or source of faith, we are tempted to place our trust in our own conceptions rather than in the Word of God. We are also tempted to regard the Word as our exclusive possession. Nevertheless, if we honestly and prayerfully strive to understand our faith and the whole of experience in the light of our faith, the probability is that our faith will be immeasurably strengthened.

Perhaps more than any contemporary theologian Niebuhr is convinced of the necessity of understanding our faith in the light of attacks upon it from the world outside the church. He is keenly aware that secular patterns of thought are a major source of heresy within the church. He is also remarkably cognizant of the fact that we fail to grasp the full implications of the gospel of God unless we understand how it "is related to what may be known about man, history, and reality through all the disciplines of culture."[32] By meeting the attacks of various secular thinkers Niebuhr has contributed greatly toward the understanding of the truth of the faith in its total dimension. What is disappointing about Niebuhr's endeavor is that although he helps to establish the relevance of the faith, he does not see that we cannot use this relevance as a means by which to persuade the unbeliever of the credibility of the faith.

In summary the heralding of the kerygma entails more than the act of preaching. We must also strive to understand the content of our proclamation so that we can grow in grace, instruct our people, and ward off heresy. In order to understand the faith fully, we must acquaint ourselves with the secular criticisms of our faith. Here I see a place for a concern that has always been present in

---

[32] Niebuhr, "Biblical Thought and Ontological Speculation in Tillich's Theology" in *The Theology of Paul Tillich*, ed. Charles W. Kegley and Robert W. Bretall (New York: Macmillan, 1952), p. 217.

apologetic theology. In contradistinction to that theology, I envisage this concern as serving the proclamation rather than an apology. We are able to understand our faith in the light of the thinking of the world and vice versa because revelation does not shatter our reason but rather liberates our reason from its servitude to sin. Through the action of the Holy Spirit our reason is sanctified and thereby empowered and impelled to interpret the content of faith as well as the whole of experience. In this way we become certain of the meaning of life and history. As Barth phrases it,

> Because as Christians we may live in the truth of Jesus Christ and therefore in the light of the knowledge of God and therefore with an illumined reason, we shall also become sure of the meaning of our own existence and of the ground and goal of all that happens.[33]

Apologetics as a Subsidiary of Kerygmatic Theology

The purpose of theological endeavor is to explicate the biblical message so that it can be proclaimed before the church and the world. Yet, as I have made clear in the last two sections, this explication entails more than an appraisal of the Bible itself. In order to understand the message in its full dimensions the theologian must make an earnest effort to scrutinize the original languages of the Bible, the cultural matrices of the biblical writings, the theological interpretations of this message through the ages, and also the history of non-Christian interpretations of life, especially those which have penetrated theological speculation.

Biblically based theologians have a threefold aim in acquainting themselves with the history of philosophy and I might add the history of religion. First of all they desire to guard against heresy in the Christian witness. One cannot truly apprehend the subtle divergences from the dogmatic norm in the history of the church and also in the contemporary situation unless one knows the sources of these divergences. Secondly, theologians must inves-

---

[33] Barth, *Dogmatics in Outline*, trans. G. T. Thomson (London: SCM Press, 1949), p. 26.

tigate the thinking of the world outside the church so that they can better appreciate the truth of the gospel. One cannot really understand the truth of faith unless one has an acute insight into the perversions of this truth not only within the sphere of the church but also in the secular culture. This is to say, one cannot truly appreciate the light unless one has also encountered the darkness. Thirdly, theologians must attempt to analyze secular thinking in order to ascertain its broken but nevertheless often profound insights. Because the truth of the gospel is imbedded in the creation of the world and of humanity, this truth can be everywhere discerned in broken form, despite human sin. Because the gospel is the criterion of as well as the judgment on all other meaning, theologians are able to appreciate the ground and goal of the meaning-patterns of the secularist. They are even allowed to incorporate certain insights of the secularist into their systems, although these insights will necessarily be purged of their ideological taint and thereby be transformed. The primary task of theologians is to make explicit what is implicit in the Bible. Yet in order to realize this end, they must strive to understand the thinking of the world outside the Bible in order to appreciate not only the truth of the Bible but also the truth in God's creation, despite the fact that this truth is in distorted form.[34] Because their reason has been enlightened by the Holy Spirit, thinking people of faith are able to see the truth in creation in its wider perspective and consequently to apprehend more fully the truth of redemption. It follows that they are also better enabled to witness to the gospel so that God might be glorified.

One facet of this attempt to utilize natural human wisdom is coping with attacks upon the Christian faith. Theologians must strive to meet such attacks not only in order to see the truth of faith more fully in the light of these attacks but also to appreciate the broken truth that can be discerned within these attacks. By exposing the ambiguities in the strictures of secular thinkers and at the same time assimilating what is valid in these strictures, theologians are thereby enabled to make the faith relevant to the existential

---

[34] *Infra*, pp. 136-137.

situation in which the church finds itself. They are able to answer the questions of the natural person, yet in such a way that these questions are negated as well as fulfilled. They are able to point to the solution for human needs, yet in a way that overthrows people's distorted interpretation of these needs.

Apologetics, as I have reconceived it, might be identified with the subsidiary task within kerygmatic theology of wrestling with non-Christian thinking, especially that thinking underlying assaults upon the faith. Something like this has been viewed as the apologetic task through the ages, but I am now giving this task a new scope and content. The apologetic enterprise no longer has for its aim the conversion of the unbeliever; instead its aim is to help the believer to integrate faith and experience. Rather than preparing one to converse with the world outside the church, it is envisaged primarily as a conversation within the church for the purpose of better understanding the faith. This transformed apologetics is conceived not as an introduction to the sermon but instead as a supplementation of the sermon. It seeks not to lay the basis for an exposition of the Bible but instead to illuminate this exposition. It does not aspire to prove or validate the faith but aims only to clarify the faith in the light of attacks upon the faith. It is not so much a vindication or defense of the faith as its illumination. It cannot even be regarded as a confirmation of the truth of faith, since this truth is self-authenticating. It seeks not to substantiate revelation in the light of experience but rather to clarify revelation in the light of experience and experience in the light of revelation. Its basic point of departure is therefore revelation, not a criterion held in common with secular thought. It takes the reality of revelation for granted and then proceeds to examine this reality in its full dimensions. Whereas traditional apologetics grappled with the problem of how revelation can be accepted, this transformed apologetics concerns itself with the problem of how revelation can be better understood once it is accepted.[35] The problem of how God's Word can be ac-

---

[35] My position on this question is very similar to that of John Dillenberger: "The church has not and does not start with the question of how God is revealed. It starts with the fact of reception and then begins to ask questions concerning the nature of this re-

cepted is not ignored; instead it is presupposed as a work of the Holy Spirit as the Spirit acts through the preaching of the Word. Apologetics as reconceived in this sense is therefore oriented no longer about an apology but rather about the heralding and explication of the message of the Bible.

Seen in this new light, apologetics can no longer be associated with what I have called "apologetic theology." The apologetic task ceases to be either an offensive or a defensive enterprise; instead it is in H. Richard Niebuhr's terminology a "confessional enterprise," carried on within the confines of the historic Christian community.[36] Its ultimate ground is revelation; its final goal is the glorification of the God who revealed Himself in Jesus Christ. Perhaps, for the purpose of clarification it would be well to substitute for "apologetics" the term "believing integration." Indeed, is not this the apologetic task seen within the framework of a kerygmatic theology? In order to appreciate the full significance of the Scriptural Word the theologian must strive to integrate faith with the whole of experience. He or she must try to see the whole of historical experience just as God sees it, i.e., in synoptic vision. At the same time we must forever be aware of our limited and also broken perspectives. Even if our reason has been sanctified, we would do well to acknowledge that the ideological taint has not been entirely eradicated. We must try to approximate the ideal of comprehending the whole of existence in the light of faith; yet we must forever recognize with Kierkegaard that an "existential system" is possible only for God.

It is well to note the differences between this type of kerygmatic theology and some of the other types. Most of the kerygmatic theologies of the past predicated a scrutiny of the thinking outside the church, but the motivation was primarily to guard against heresy. My motivation is not only negative but also positive. I see the Spirit of God at work in the history of philosophy and also in the history of religion. I contend that despite the fact that the thinking

---

ception in relation to all other problems of knowledge." Dillenberger, *God Hidden and Revealed* (Philadelphia: Muhlenberg Press, 1953), p. 177. Cf. pp. 144-185.

[36] *Supra*, pp. 9-10.

of secularists is distorted by their rebellion against God, God nevertheless acts upon their thinking even if this be against their inclinations. A theologian is therefore enabled to incorporate certain insights in the history of philosophy so long as he or she divorces these insights from their secular context and subsumes them under the criterion of revelation. There is a risk and also a necessity in this enterprise, as I shall make clear in the concluding section. Calvin is among the few kerygmatic theologians who hold that secular philosophy can make some type of contribution to a theological system. Karl Barth advocates a study of philosophy, but he refuses to allow philosophical categories to penetrate the realm of theology.[37] Perhaps his keen awareness of the dangers in such a procedure has rendered him incapable of perceiving its real possibilities. My position must be seen as especially contrary to that of the early Barth, who at that time tended to depreciate the role of sanctified reason. Barth and the other crisis theologians were then too much under the influence of existentialist philosophy to take into sufficient consideration the internal work of the Spirit. I believe that the kerygmatic theologian, in order to draw out the full meaning of the biblical Word, must relate creatively to the entire compass of the history of philosophy and religion, and this enterprise signalizes the rebirth of apologetics, but it is an apologetics in a new role and context.

As I have noted previously, my reevaluation of apologetics involves a transformation of its original purpose; it also entails a transformation of the traditional as well as of the newer apologetic methods. Nearly all of these apologetic methods serve to compromise the faith, since their aim is to prepare the way for the conversion of the unbeliever; consequently they seek for common ground with unbelief for purposes of dialogue. Yet most of these apologetic

---

[37] Barth also sees little that is of positive worth in the history of religion: "Religion is the concern...of godless man." Barth sees the history of religion as the history of man's idolatrous presumption. But does not this history also manifest the work of common grace? See Karl Barth, "God's Revelation as the Dissolution of Religion" in *Die Kirchliche Dogmatik* (Zollikon-Zürich: Evangelischer Verlag, 1948), 1(2): 304-397.

methods when oriented about the task of faith seeking understanding can be of some value.

I have not said much concerning the traditional proofs for the existence of God, since Niebuhr does not take them seriously. Yet I believe that there is something valid in every one of these proofs, but this "something" can be discerned only from a kerygmatic perspective. The ontological proof for the existence of God can be criticized from a biblical viewpoint on the grounds that sinful humanity is incapable of conceiving the holy God. Yet when this proof is regarded no longer as a proof but instead as an illumination of what Christians already know to be true in their experience, then it has a real albeit modest place within the theological enterprise. The Christian, unlike the non-Christian, has personally encountered the perfect being, and can therefore know of His existence as well as certain of His attributes. A similar analysis can be made of the cosmological argument. This argument can only validate the idea of a first cause when its appeal is made to natural reason (and even this has been questioned). On the other hand, when this argument is oriented about a reason sanctified by the Holy Spirit, it appears convincing. The teleological proof can also be adopted by the kerygmatic theologian so long as it is treated not as a proof but rather as an amplification of what we already know to be true. Paley's analogy of the watch and the watchmaker can be appreciated by Christians in every age as an excellent statement of how design in nature illumines the Mind that is operating within and behind nature. In his *Dialogues Concerning Natural Religion* Hume showed that the teleological argument in its traditional role can be successfully countered.[38] Yet, when this argument is viewed not as a theoretical proof but rather as an elucidation of the faith of a Christian, then it can be readily incorporated by kerygmatic theologians.

The moral argument for the existence of God has been in vogue throughout the ages, but it has been especially prominent

---

[38] David Hume, *Dialogues Concerning Natural Religion*, ed. Norman Kemp Smith (New York: Thomas Nelson, 1947).

among modern Protestants (both liberal and orthodox). C.S. Lewis in his seminal book *Mere Christianity* gives an excellent statement of the moral argument.[39] He demonstrates the objective existence of a moral law and then tries to show that the Mind behind the moral law can be none other than the God who revealed Himself in Jesus Christ. Here again we might say that this is convincing to those who are seeking the truth revealed by God, but to the person in sin this argument can be questioned. Such a person doubts the plausibility of this argument and the other arguments for the existence of God not because they necessarily contradict the logical structure of reason (although this is what some will contend) but rather because the God they point to opposes our self-seeking will. I concur with Immanuel Kant that while the moral argument does not furnish a theoretical proof of God it does provide a practical insight into the nature of God once we make a decision.

Arguments supporting the divinity of Christ on the basis of biblical prophecy have been demolished by the higher criticism of the Bible. It has now been shown that the prophets were not always accurate in foretelling future events. Even when the argument of prophecy had considerable weight among the Christian intelligentsia, it had little if any effect upon the non-Christian world. Yet I believe that although Christians can no longer use this argument in its original form, it can be appropriated in a new form and in a new role. Alan Richardson states this new form in his *Christian Apologetics*. He maintains that whereas we can no longer conceive of prophecy as a prediction of events yet to come, we can reconceive biblical prophecy in terms of a creative insight into events that can be regarded as types or anticipations of the Christ event. Because the determinative events attested to in the Bible culminate in the Incarnation, the insights of the prophets concerning this revelatory pattern help to illumine and clarify biblical faith.[40] What Richardson does not adequately consider is that this illumination is

---

[39] C.S. Lewis, *Mere Christianity* (New York: Macmillan,1943).

[40] See Alan Richardson, *Christian Apologetics* (New York: Harper & Brothers, 1947), pp. 177-201.

of benefit only to the person who acknowledges the revelation of Christ.

The argument for the divinity of Christ and also for the existence of a supernatural God on the basis of biblical miracles must be treated in a similar manner. Niebuhr is unabashedly critical of miracle apologetics, and his criticisms are justified in so far as this type of apologetics purports to prove the truth of faith. If the strange phenomena attested to in the New Testament in particular are to be seen as acts of a God who stands beyond the realm of relativity and contingency, then they can be known to be such only through the eyes of faith. Faith does not preclude a critical analysis of the miracle stories; indeed, it demands it, for anything that is objectively accessible must be subjected to criticism. On the other hand, the person who believes will find, on the basis of a critical appraisal, that some of the miracles are an integral part of the Christian message. This person will find that they serve to illumine the divinity and supernatural character of Christ, but by no means do they prove His divinity. One of the latest works on this subject which I heartily recommend is C.S. Lewis' *Miracles*.[41] I would take exception only to those sections in which he makes an appeal to the non-Christian and thereby obscures the basis for assenting to the gospel, viz., the assurance of forgiveness.

The method of correlation, which has been popularized in various forms by Niebuhr, Tillich, and Brunner, can also be of service when reconceived as a part of the general kerygmatic enterprise. There is a type of correlation between Christian revelation and secular philosophy, but this correlation is not obvious. There is a type of correlation because the Spirit of God works in and through the reasoning process of the natural person, sometimes even against that person's will. It is not obvious because this operation of the Holy Spirit is obscured and distorted by the rebellion of sin. The Christian apologist can baptize certain insights of secular thought and thereby relate them to the Christian answer. This relation entails not only the fulfillment of these insights but also their

---

[41] C.S. Lewis, *Miracles* (1947; reprint London: Geoffrey Bles, 1952).

negation. The revelatory predilections of the insights and questions of the natural person can be discerned only by the one who is aware of the theological answer. The method of correlation is therefore valid only as an interpretation of secular philosophy within the theological circle. There can be no meeting ground in ultimate matters between those who stand within the circle and those who stand outside.

When seen within the confines of the kerygmatic enterprise, the eristical approach can also be appreciated. "Eristics" as we remember is the method of attack, the attempt to undermine the position of our adversary. Niebuhr's basic approach is "eristical," since his aim is to undercut the meaning patterns of his hearers and thereby lead them into "creative despair." I have said that theology must be neither a defensive nor an offensive enterprise but rather a "confessional enterprise." Yet this confession, which is carried on within the theological circle, will necessarily entail a critique of secular thought. Such a critique is addressed not to non-Christians so much as to Christians with the purpose of helping them to understand their faith and also to strengthen their faith. St. Paul here affirms the eristical aspect of the kerygmatic task: "We destroy arguments and every proud obstacle to the knowledge of God, and take every thought captive to obey Christ."[42] There is, of course, the general stricture of the church upon the idolatrous pretension of humanity, which is directed both to the church and to the world. Yet this general attack upon "sin" cannot be regarded as apologetics in the traditional sense of the word, since there is no appeal to sinful reason, only an appeal to the Holy Ghost. Niebuhr's attempt, even in his sermons, to expose the contradictions in the unbelieving mind is an appeal to this mind and presupposes that it is capable of rising above these contradictions and illusions. This is eristics in the traditional sense of the word. The general attack upon sin cannot be understood as "eristics" in either the traditional or the transformed sense, since it consists in confronting people in sin with their guilt and misery rather than persuading them to acknowledge

---

[42] 2 Cor. 10:5.

the discrepancies in their reasoning. I would consider the general attack upon sin as an integral part of the evangelical proclamation.

There are other apologetic arguments (e.g., the mystical and the pragmatic), but my analysis has provided a sufficient picture of how such arguments are transformed when viewed as a supplement rather than an introduction to the sermon. As soon as these arguments assume a new role, viz., that of amplifying rather than establishing the truth of faith, they must be given a slightly different presentation and sometimes also a different content. The reason for this change is that they are no longer intended to appeal to the perspective of natural reason but instead presuppose the perspective of faith. These arguments illumine the intrinsic rationality of faith, although only the person whose reason has been liberated from its bondage to ideological forces can appreciate this rationality. By analyzing the secular thought of the time, theologians can demonstrate how the problems that beset the thinking of the natural person can be resolved only by revelation. We are thereby able to show the relevance of Christian faith to the contemporary situation. On the other hand, if we attempt to use this relevance as a basis on which to establish the credibility of the faith, we then revert to apologetic theology. For example, we can show how the intentions of the Marxist to transcend the ideological taint can be realized only by participation in the New Being, which lies beyond the realm of contingency. Once we try to prove to the Marxist, however, that the latter's efforts can be fulfilled only within the Christian community, we then lose sight of the ground of faith, viz., the Holy Spirit, who alone can convert and transform the mind of the unbeliever.

The main divergence between my reevaluation of the apologetic task and Niebuhr's lies in the purpose ascribed to this task. Niebuhr sees the immediate aim of apologetics as the validation of the basic insights of the faith, which ostensibly establishes the relevance of the faith. Its ultimate aim is to move the non-Christian toward a decision: "The apologetic task has the object of inducing the confession: 'Lord, to whom shall we go? Thou hast the words of eternal life.'"[43] I see the apologetic task as an attempt to illumine and clarify the insights of faith so that the Christian can understand the faith more fully and witness to the faith more effectively. I believe that the apologetic task must be envisaged in terms of supplementing faith and the means of faith rather than of bringing faith.[44] Apologetics must be treated as a subsidiary task within the broader task of faith seeking understanding. The glimpses of truth that a faithful or enlightened reason can uncover illumine the faith and in some cases even strengthen the faith, but they cannot be said to validate or confirm the faith. The principle of validation is given by the Holy Spirit; this is to say that it is integral to faith itself. In contradistinction to Niebuhr I do not believe that the truth of faith can be defended or recommended. It can only be illumined and clarified. I might acknowledge that the truth of faith can be supported by insights drawn from experience, provided that this "support" be regarded as derivative – resting upon the illumination of the Holy Spirit. I will also allow that various affirmations that are drawn from this truth can be defended and recommended, yet only within the sphere of the church. This is to say, there is room for polemics, but not for apologetics as this has been traditionally conceived. Like Niebuhr I believe that the insights of faith must be related to the insights of culture. In opposition to Niebuhr I contend that the truth of faith is self-authenticating; therefore the purpose of the apologetic task is not to validate or prove the faith before the world with the hope of inducing commitment but rather to bring out the intrinsic rationality of faith within the church so that God's will might be more effectively known and proclaimed.

---

[43] Reinhold Niebuhr, "Intellectual Autobiography", *Reinhold Niebuhr: His Religious, Social and Political Thought*, ed. Charles W. Kegley and Robert Bretall, (New York: Macmillan, 1956), p. 17.

[44] To be sure a kerygmatic apologetics might indirectly be instrumental in bringing faith, since it can help one to preach more effectively, and the sermon is the means of faith. Yet what is important in understanding the difference between my position and Niebuhr's is that I believe that the aim of apologetics, even the ultimate aim, is not to *bring faith* but simply to *make known* the faith. The Holy Spirit converts some through the sermon, but He also hardens and blinds others.

Niebuhr himself more than once concedes the fact that experience appears to validate various views of life depending upon one's presuppositions. At a very early date he opined: "Life is so complex that it may validate at the same time the theories of one who lives upon the assumption that it is 'an eddy of meaningless dust' and of another who believes that 'all things work together for good to them that love God.'"[45] More recently he contends that "we are confronted with evidence" that the biblical perspective is more true to the facts of life than alternative perspectives.[46] But at another place he says that "the commitment tends to select the evidence."[47] In his recently published "Intellectual Autobiography" he pictures one's guiding principles as "spectacles" that color but do not fully control experience.[48] For the most part Niebuhr seems to be saying that although our commitment predisposes us to look at the world in a certain way, our experience in the world will validate or invalidate this commitment. I would agree that in many cases one's experience is decisive in determining the validity of one's commitment. But in the case of Christian faith, which is qualitatively different from other faiths, this is not true. Christian faith or commitment is a gift of God, and its ground is therefore unconditional and absolute. The unconditional cannot be validated by that which is conditioned, for this would be a contradiction in terms. The content of Christian faith is none other than the Word of God, and this Word cannot be vindicated or validated by the broken insights of humanity. It is itself the measure and criterion of all meaning; it therefore cannot be measured or judged by that which is lesser than itself. The Word of God can be illumined by the insights of culture in so far as these insights are in part guided and directed by the Word. But since only an illumined or sanctified reason can discern the subtle relation between the Word and the in-

---

[45] Reinhold Niebuhr, "Shall We Proclaim the Truth or Search for It?" *The Christian Century*, 42, no. 11 (March 12, 1925), p. 345.

[46] *The Self and the Dramas of History* (New York: Charles Scribner's Sons, 1955), p. 71.

[47] "Christ vs. Socrates," *The Saturday Review*, 37 (Dec. 18, 1954), p. 39.

[48] *Reinhold Niebuhr: His Religious, Social and Political Thought*, ed. Charles W. Kegley and Robert W. Bretall, p. 16.

sights of culture, it is a source of confusion to speak of these insights as validating or proving the Word.

Karl Barth has made a helpful contribution to this discussion. He draws a distinction between the terms "illustration" and "interpretation." Both of these purport to say the same thing in other words, but "illustration" unduly stresses the "other words" and thereby amounts to saying something else. According to Barth the truth of faith can be interpreted, but not illustrated, for this would mean that "it is calling for support, strength, and confirmation of one's language about it from a source other than itself."[49] The attempt to illustrate the insights of faith is apologetics both in the traditional and the Niebuhrian senses. It indicates "a failure in proper trust in revelation with respect to its own power of self-evidence."[50] Whereas the method of illustration places its confidence in "the capacity of reason for revelation," the method of interpretation places its confidence in "the power of revelation over reason."[51] This is to say, God's Word is capable of supporting Himself. It is proper for the minister who is a servant of the Word to proclaim, interpret, and meditate upon the Word, but it is presumptuous for that person to attempt to illustrate or support the Word.

Apologetics as an Aid in Witnessing

It would be well to consider how a reconceived apologetics or what I have called "believing integration" can help one to witness intelligibly and forcefully. I believe that the two main components of an intelligible witness are fidelity to the kerygma and penetration of the cultural situation. The first concerns the content of our witness. We must continually seek to purify our thinking and language so that it is God's Word and not our word that is heard. To speak

---

[49] Barth, *The Doctrine of the Word of God*, trans. G.T. Thomson (Edinburgh: T. & T. Clark, 1949), p. 396.

[50] *Ibid.*

[51] *Ibid.*, p. 392.

the pure kerygma is of course not a human possibility, but this should nevertheless be our ideal. The second component concerns the structure of our witness. It is my contention that ministers should endeavor to formulate their witness in terms familiar to their hearers. Just as Christ became in all things as we are, yet without sin, so we should try to incarnate our message in the situation in which our hearers find themselves, yet striving to keep this message free from the sin-tainted patterns of meaning that infect the situation. Karl Barth recommends that we should convey the message in the "language of the newspaper," i.e., in the language of the "common man."[52] At the same time, we must translate this language back into the "language of Canaan," for the form and content of the Bible cannot be permanently extricated. To incarnate our message in the situation and yet to keep this message pure is again not a human possibility, but it nevertheless must be our goal or ideal. In the last analysis only the Holy Spirit can make our witness truly intelligible, since only the Spirit can convey the real kerygma and only the Spirit can penetrate the situation.

Apologetics in this new perspective enables us to hold to the basic content of the faith by helping us to understand this content in the light of attacks upon it from the world outside the church. We who bear witness must of course expound the biblical text in the light of the kerygma and not of secular thought. At the same time, the kerygma itself throws light upon secular attacks on the faith and thereby enables us to see the faith in relation to unbelief both within and outside the church. By seeing the biblical message in contradistinction to the thinking of the world we are thereby enabled to guard against syncretism in our witness.

Reinhold Niebuhr has made a signal contribution to this phase of apologetics by contrasting the Christian position with other positions, even though his aim is not primarily the illumination of the faith, but rather its validation. Just as Calvin at times exposed the contradictions within the secular thought of his time, so Niebuhr does the same in our time, only on a much greater scale

---

[52] Karl Barth, *Dogmatics in Outline*, pp. 32, 33.

and with much more precision. The principal difference is that Calvin makes it much more clear than Niebuhr that the analysis of secular thought, whether it be positive or negative, can be of benefit only to the Christian. Calvin rightly holds that only a reason enlightened by the Holy Spirit can appreciate the woeful discrepancies as well as the grains of truth in the thinking of the natural person.

Apologetics also aids the task of evangelism by enabling Christians to incarnate their message in the cultural situation. This incarnation does not entail a synthesis or even a correlation with secular thought; rather it predicates its negation. At the same time Christians will utilize the language and imagery of the cultural situation, but they will give this language and imagery a new meaning and direction. This is to say that in their attempt to relate the message to the culture they will transform or "baptize" the thought forms that are indigenous to their hearers. Because there are many risks and dangers in this enterprise, it is appropriate to spend some time in explicating its scope and content.

It is possible for the Christian to baptize the imagery of the culture for two reasons. First of all, the "imago Dei" still exists within every human being, despite the fact of sin. The general revelation in creation has been obscured by human perversity, but it still remains. Secondly, God continually works in and through our fallen social environment. This is what Calvin called "common grace." Such a doctrine is firmly rooted in the New Testament. It is reflected in these words of Jesus: "He makes his sun rise on the evil and on the good, and sends rain on the just and on the unjust."[53] Everywhere the Spirit of God presses upon the thinking of sinful men and women and at times diverts their thinking toward the cross, even against their basic predilections. It is therefore possible for Christians to appropriate certain insights of the secularist, for they are able with an enlightened reason to discern the revelatory pattern of meaning that these insights reflect even though this pattern is denied by the basic philosophy of the secularist.

---

[53] Matt. 5:45.

Although God is at work in the fallen world of humanity, there can be no common area of understanding between Christian faith and secular thought. Our rebellion against God has so obfuscated the "imago Dei" that our capacity to seek and know God has been irretrievably impaired. There is still a basic relation between God and humanity, but this relation is now perverted. At the same time, it must be said that this perversion is not equally manifest in all areas of human thinking. I agree with Brunner that the disruption caused by sin is most manifest in the center of human existence, which concerns our relationship with God and his being as a person. The farther away anything lies from this center, the less is the disturbance of sin felt, "and the less difference is there between knowing as a believer or as an unbeliever."[54] Yet even where the disturbance is at its minimum, i.e., in the sphere of mathematics and the exact sciences, the ideological taint is still evident. Although both Christian and non-Christian perceive the same facts, they interpret these facts from a different metaphysical position and thereby read into the facts slightly and sometimes obviously different meanings. Again, even where the disturbance is at its maximum, i.e., in the sphere of theology, the natural person is still able to arrive at some valid insights that reflect the Word of God, but such insights will necessarily be accidental.

It would be well to mention some of the insights in secular thought that lend themselves to appropriation by Christian theology. The doctrine of the impassiblity of God, which dominated most of classical philosophy, contains the valid insight that God cannot be contingent upon the world of becoming. When Christians incorporate this insight, of course, they will take pains to divorce it from the conception of the Unmoved Mover (Aristotle) and subsume it under the Living God who gives Himself in love. Kant's recognition of the structural limitations of reason can be appreciated by the theologian as reflecting the biblical position regarding human finitude. His doctrine of radical evil can also be ap-

---

[54] Emil Brunner, *Revelation and Reason*, trans. Olive Wyon (Philadelphia: Westminster Press, 1946), p. 383.

preciated as reflecting the biblical doctrine of sin. In both cases Kant falls short of grasping the full impact of either human finitude or sin, and any assimilation of his insights along this line on the part of the theologian necessarily entails a transformation of meaning. Hegel's contention that an idea must become concrete if it is not to remain impotent faintly resembles the Christian doctrine of incarnation. Marx's insight concerning the ideological cast of human reasoning and also Nietzsche's perception of the distortion of conscience by the passions reflect the Christian doctrine of the defilement of the "imago Dei" by sin. Whitehead's analysis of religious experience as consisting in a movement from God the void to God the enemy to God the companion can be said to reflect the Christian experience of the wrath and love of God as one encounters the law and gospel respectively.[55] Certain insights in secular philosophy that might be deemed revelatory can be appropriated by the Christian so long as they are given a new context and direction. There can be no common court of judgment with secular thought in matters of ultimate concern because this thought is necessarily oriented about the self-seeking human will, which stands in diametrical opposition to the will of God. At the same time, because God works in and through the reasoning process of secular people even against their rebellious inclinations, certain insights can be discerned in their thinking that point to God's Word and thereby lend themselves to "baptism" by the theologian.

There is a risk and a necessity in the baptism of secular thought forms and imagery. Theologians take a risk in this enterprise because they might very well incorporate not only the secular imagery but also its ideological meaning. We are commanded to incarnate our message in the cultural situation, but it is incumbent on us to make every effort to avoid a synthesis or even a correlation with the meaning patterns that pervade the situation. We are to become in all things as our hearers, yet striving to keep ourselves free from sin, including the sin within thought. Theologians cannot

---

[55] Alfred North Whitehead, *Religion in the Making* (New York: Macmillan, 1926), pp. 16-17.

therefore really enter into the existential situation of their hearers; they can only confront the situation with the biblical kerygma. They must use language and imagery indigenous to the situation and yet fill these earthen vessels with new meaning, meaning that can be known only through the action of the Holy Spirit. Theologians must forever walk the knife's edge between synthesis and obscurantism. They can partly avoid these pitfalls if they place themselves in the situation of their hearers and then try to imagine how well they (with an enlightened reason) would be able to understand the proclamation. In this way it is perhaps possible for them to eschew any synthesis with an alien philosophy as well as an obscurantism that completely isolates their preaching from their hearers.

In order to guard against any fusion with cultural or natural wisdom, we would do well to enumerate certain principles that might help us in determining the selection of the symbols and thought forms of culture for purposes of appropriation. First of all, theologians should select imagery that is indigenous to the situation. This is to say, these images must be familiar to our hearers. Secondly, they must be appropriate to the reality to which they are being applied. This can be partly determined on the basis of whether they are analogous to the symbols baptized by the prophets and apostles and also whether they are held in high enough esteem to be applied to the transcendent world. For example, the symbol "king" although found in the Bible and congruous with some other biblical symbols cannot easily be made to refer to God in those areas where people have suffered under the heavy hand of monarchy. Even though this symbol has biblical overtones it can only be incorporated in a biblical theology with significant alterations in meaning. We must always take care never to place false scandals before our hearers lest the authentic scandal be obscured. German theologian Karl Heim baptized the Nazi symbol "Leader" by referring to Jesus as the "Leader."[56] This symbol was relevant at the time of his writing (1930's), but it has now lost much of its power be-

---

[56] See Karl Heim, *The Church of Christ and the Problems of the Day* (London: Nisbet & Co., 1936), pp. 99-124; and E.L. Allen, *Jesus Our Leader: A Guide To The Thought of Karl Heim* (London: Hodder & Stoughton, 1948).

cause Nazism has been vanquished. Again, the theologian must not incorporate any secular symbol unless it can be meaningfully subsumed under the biblical symbols. Finally, there is the pragmatic test of whether the Holy Spirit appears to utilize these symbols in bringing our hearers to repentance.

We might also list certain criteria that determine the use of the baptized symbols. First of all, such symbols must be subordinated to the biblical story. Only by directly relating these symbols to analogous symbols in the Bible are we able to fill these symbols with new meaning. Secondly, we must continually make a conscious effort to differentiate the new meaning associated with these symbols from their original or generative meaning. Many of the medieval theologians were aware of the often radical difference between the secular and theological meanings of the terms they employed, but because they did not always make this difference clear, they were unable to prevent a synthesis with secular thought.

The guiding imagery of the Bible is for the most part baptized imagery, i.e., imagery incorporated from the culture. Indeed, the biblical writers were compelled to speak in the language of their own time, but they made a conscious attempt to transform this language in the light of the gospel. For example, *kairos* in the mind of Aristotle signifies "the good in the category of time." If a special moment of time is good for the fulfillment of something, this moment is its *kairos*. But for Aristotle and other secularists time itself has no *kairos*. *Kairos* as employed in the New Testament, however, signifies the fulfillment of time itself. *Telos* for Aristotle signifies the immanent aim of the life-process. Paul utilizes this term but gives it a horizontal or eschatological meaning rather than a vertical meaning. For Homer *charis* (grace) means an act of kindness, especially as shown by a superior to an inferior. In the New Testament *charis* means God's favor toward people contrary to their deserving. *Metanoia* (repentance) for the Greeks meant changing one's mind. For the apostles *metanoia* signifies a complete change of life. *Parousia* (presence, appearance) for Plato meant the presence of the good that appears in all things and yet is beyond all things. For Christians this word refers to the second coming, i.e., to a unique historical or transhistorical event. Again, *aletheia* (truth) for the Greeks meant penetrating to the level of reality that is hidden to the natural world view and that can be discovered only by methodological knowledge. For Christians *aletheia* points to the practical certainty that follows something that happened – God becoming incarnate in human flesh. *Aletheia* is participation in a transforming event rather than something to be simply believed.[57]

There are certain symbols in contemporary life that lend themselves to appropriation by the Christian theologian. The symbol "crisis," for example, has very potent connotations in the modern world. If the theologian baptizes this symbol, however, these connotations are thereby transformed. For Christians "crisis" in its deepest context signifies not the turning point of civilization or even the turning point of a person's life as such but rather the turning point in our relation with God. Again, the symbol "freedom" when employed for theological purposes is filled with a meaning quite different from that which it generically embodies. For the natural person "freedom," at least in our social order, means the opportunity to pursue one's own happiness. When seen within the context of the Bible, "freedom" signifies liberation from soul-destroying powers and the possibility to sacrifice the self for the welfare of one's neighbor and for the glory of God. "Anxiety" has many popular and scientific connotations, but in the light of the gospel it means something quite different. In philosophical circles it refers to the experience of one's finitude; in psychological circles it connotes the experience of being unwilling to accept one's finitude. Within the theological realm it refers primarily to the experience of being incapable of recognizing one's sin and guilt in the sight of God. Theologians will retain the original and popular meaning of every symbol that they appropriate, but they will give the symbol another and deeper meaning when it is used within the sphere of ultimate concern.

---

[57] See a pertinent discussion of conflicting Greek and Christian meanings of some key New Testament words in Paul Tillich, *The Protestant Era*, trans. James Luther Adams (Chicago: University of Chicago Press, 1948), pp. 27-31.

Theologians must take care not to employ the secular terms that they adopt as apologetical devices in the traditional sense. This is to say, theologians in their sermons must not try to use secular terms and categories for purposes of establishing common ground with their hearers in order to convince them of the reasonableness of the faith. We must remember that the terms that we appropriate are transformed in the light of the gospel. The meaning that they embody in a sermon or theological work is qualitatively different from their generic or popular meaning. Therefore these terms cannot be made the basis for an appeal to the world. It is right, for example, for the theologian to appropriate the category "freedom" in order to describe the state of the person under grace. We take a grave risk, however, if we attempt to syncretize the popular and baptized meanings of this term in order to lead or direct the unbeliever into the sphere of belief. If we try to demonstrate that Christian freedom is a superior kind of freedom or the highest type of freedom, we are subsuming the kerygmatic meaning within a secular framework of meaning and thereby subverting the kerygmatic meaning. The language of theology can be interpreted only in the context of God's reconciling work on the cross, not in its popular or secular context. Faithful theologians will constantly relate the gospel to the thinking of the world, but they do this not in order to build a bridge between the world and the gospel but in order to confront the world with the gospel. They seek to understand the cultural situation in the light of the gospel so that they can proclaim the gospel intelligibly, i.e., in terms indigenous to the situation and yet grounded in the meaning of the gospel. They desire to know about the ideology of the culture so that they can be certain that what they proclaim is the gospel and not the ideology.

Apologetics when reconceived as a part of the kerygmatic enterprise can be of immeasurable value in the task of witnessing. By enabling one to understand one's faith better in the light of attacks upon it, the apologetic enterprise helps one to convey the truth of faith. By acquainting theologians with the thinking of the natural person, especially thinking that goes counter to Christian faith, apologetics enables them to guard against syncretism in their witness. Again, by making a thorough analysis of the existential situation in which people find themselves, the apologetic enterprise helps theologians to confront the situation with the biblical message while at the same time ensuring that their message will rise above ideology. By acknowledging the work of God in the thinking of the world outside the church, the apologetic enterprise enables theologians to baptize certain revelatory insights within secular thought thereby making it possible for them to give their message a concrete and tangible structure. The immediate aim of a kerygmatic apologetics is the clarification and illumination of the content of faith by seeking to understand this faith in the light of the thinking of the world outside the church. Its ultimate aim is the glorification of God by means of the intelligible proclamation of the biblical kerygma.

Epilogue

Reinhold Niebuhr has made an insightful and admirable attempt to reevaluate the apologetic task in the light of the biblical revelation. Like many other contemporary theologians he is severely critical of the apologetics of the past, especially that which tried to conform Christian faith to the modern idea of progress. He presents a credible case that these new forms of apologetics "were content to teach the modern, rather than the Christian, faith if only they would be allowed to tell the story through the pictures and symbols, the concepts and images drawn from the Scripture, and tortured to yield the same plan of salvation in which the modern man already believed."[1] Niebuhr's concern is to safeguard the uniqueness of the insights of the Bible and at the same time establish their relevance to the contemporary situation. My position has been that Niebuhr does not completely eschew the errors of traditional and modern apologetics in that he appeals both to the biblical message and to the meaning-orientations of the culture. For the most part, his appeal is to the *justitia originalis* or the human conscience, which he denominates as the "point of contact" between reason and revelation. I have tried to show on the basis of Scripture that sin has eradicated any kind of contact between God and humanity that has epistemological significance. I have argued that Niebuhr does not fully appreciate the extent of the disruption caused by sin. He does not acknowledge that sin has incapacitated us both for seeking and for apprehending the gospel. Because he believes that the natural person is capable of responding to God's revelation in nature and in history, he builds his case on the supposed capacity of a searching humanity to find and know God. He is thereby led to orient his witness more about criteria held in common with secular thought than about the Word. In a signifi-

---

[1] *Faith and History*, p. 32.

cant work in his later years he takes for his point of departure the human self rather than the revelation of Christ.[2] He tries to prepare the way for the acceptance of the biblical message by leading his hearers into creative despair. He maintains that an eristical apologia can be a means of grace that can bring our hearers to repentance. I believe on the basis of the Bible that only the proclamation of the gospel is the means by which God has chosen to implant His wisdom in the hearts of people. This proclamation consists in both a word of judgment and a word of grace, but this word of judgment, which undercuts our idolatry in the light of the cross, must be differentiated from a sophisticated analysis of the contradictions and antinomies of reason with which Niebuhr concerns himself.

Although I cannot follow Niebuhr in his proposed strategy to prepare the way for faith, I am sympathetic with his concern to relate the faith creatively to all areas of culture and experience. I have tried to reconceive apologetics in such a way as to do justice to both the biblical doctrines of sin and grace and the biblical and Niebuhrian concern to witness intelligibly. I have envisaged the apologetic task as one aspect of the general task of faith seeking understanding. Its purpose is no longer that of convincing or persuading the unbeliever of the credibility of the faith; rather it aims to help the believer to understand the faith better so that he or she can testify more intelligibly and responsibly for the glory of God. This transformed apologetics does not deal with the question of how reason can accept or validate revelation; instead it concerns itself with how a reason enlightened by revelation can understand the deeper implications of both faith and experience. Niebuhr would not call this apologetics. I have retained this term, since my theology includes at least one concern of the apologetics of the past and that is to answer secular attacks leveled upon the faith (even if this answering is not intended to be addressed primarily to the unbeliever for the purpose of conversion). Yet since most if not all of traditional apologetics has been geared to the persuasion or conversion

---

[2] *The Self and the Dramas of History* (1955). This book signifies not a departure from Niebuhr's earlier stance but a reaffirmation of themes going back even to his liberal period. Throughout his theology Niebuhr gives anthropology priority over Christology.

of the cultured despisers of religion, my retention of the term "apologetics" might well be questioned. Whatever the case might be, I believe that the endeavor to integrate faith and experience on the basis of faith and within the circle of faith contains all that is valid in the apologetics of the past and also opens up new horizons for a kerygmatic type of theology.

www.ingramcontent.com/pod-product-compliance
Lightning Source LLC
Chambersburg PA
CBHW051941160426
43198CB00013B/2249